Mary Jo,
May you see
always the beauty
in the scar.
~ Tami

FINDING PURPOSE
IN THE HEALING

Beautiful
Scars

RHONDA McCOY & TAMI BURTRON

This book is lovingly dedicated to our families. Thank you for the encouragement and selfless support throughout this journey.

Contents

Preface

**You are altogether beautiful, my darling;
there is no flaw in you.**

—Song of Solomon 4:7 NIV

We all have them.

Scars.

Wounds that healed and now each time we see them, we remember.

The stories that made the wound that made the scar. Whether it was tripping while playing hopscotch in second grade, falling off our bike at age 12, a family car accident or surgery because of an angry appendix. We have permanent reminders of traumas we went through.

We also carry scars that no one can see. The ones that have molded our heart to be shaped differently. The ones that still hurt when triggered. The ones that do not seem to heal. We all have them. Broken homes. Shattered relationships. Cancer. Abuse. Infertility. A mental health crisis. A long distance move. Death of a loved one. Poor self-esteem. Rejection.

Walk along this journey with us as we share moments, days, and seasons in which our lives were far from idyllic. Somehow along the way, we found joy was a choice of the heart.

While your story may look a little different from ours, we all must face challenges, devastation, and brokenness at some point. Pain, wounds, and scars are the common denominators. We really are alike.

As you read through these stories, we hope you can reflect on how it may apply to you or someone in your circle. Perhaps you would like to pick up a pen and your favorite notebook to journal your thoughts and takeaways.

Our prayer is that you find yourself within the pages of this book and that you are filled with hope and perspective. We trust that you will relate to the stories, memories, lessons learned, triumphs, tragedies, hopes, do-overs, dreams, and yes, even the scars.

Beautiful life changing scars.

Rhonda & Tami

Introduction

Sometimes the thing you never would choose for your life, chooses you for a reason. And the thing that you'd never pick, picks you to become brave. And sometimes you get what you need by walking through what you never wanted. And the thing you never wanted may turn out to be the thing you most need.

—Ann Voskamp

Rhonda: In January 2020, I received a text message from my sweet friend Tami. It said something like "Hey, when can you talk? I have a very bizarre idea that I want to run by you!"
In the few days between that text and when we talked on the phone, I thought about what this might be about. The first thing that came to my mind was that it had something to do with writing.

Tami: I was dying to share this crazy bright idea that I had been thinking about for some time. Assuming my friend Rhonda would think I've lost my mind since I'm not a writer, I nervously shared that we should write a book together. Oh dear, what have I done? She actually said YES!

Rhonda: It only took a few minutes of hearing her heart and I knew that I was all in! We made plans to get together, came up with a title, and started digging into the world of writing a book.

Tami: On March 4, 2020, two Midwest girls with words on their heart traveled from Indiana and Iowa to meet halfway in Illinois. Giddy, clueless, excited, and embracing the unknown, we set out on this new adventure. Meshing two worlds of life's struggles and challenges, we broke out the pen and paper—okay it was our phones and computers. Nonetheless, God began to show up and we knew then that He was in it and all we needed to do was trust the pen in His hand. He was certainly writing the story, as you will see. He had already gone before us.

Rhonda: I love coffee and all things coffee shops so we researched and found a few that would be our landing spots for a couple of days as we got to work. Zion in downtown Peoria was the first place on the list. With a coffee and hot tea in hand, we spent hours outlining this book. One of the meanings of the name Zion is "a holy place". I can tell you that we felt every bit of that as we poured through the stories that would eventually make up this book you are now holding. God was so present in those first moments, and we decided early on we would follow His lead.

Tami: We departed with smiles on our faces knowing and believing something amazing had just been born. I remember shedding a few tears on that three-hour drive home. Tears of gratefulness that God had chosen us. Tears of joy that this was really happening. The scars that once brought pain looked a little bit different on this day. There was no looking back.

Rhonda and Tami: And so, it began...

> **He is close to the brokenhearted and binds up their wounds.**
>
> —Psalm 147:3 NIV

Heartache to Hope

God calls you to the place where your deep gladness and the world's deep hunger meet.

—Fredrich Beuchner

I am no stranger to heartache.

My husband Everett and I had been married six years when a doctor abrasively said that we would have a lifetime of infertility. There was no possibility of a biological child.

We took the news relatively well. We had always talked about fostering or adopting even while we were dating, so we just assumed our Plan B was now God's Plan A.

Life took over for the next twelve years as we advanced in our careers which included a move to Northern

Virginia and then to Alabama.

After living in the Birmingham area for a couple of years, we just knew it was time. It was that now or never feeling.

I left my 23-year career as an ophthalmic technician to go through the foster/adoptive classes and prepare to hopefully become a first-time mom... at age 42.

I remember a nagging question that rose within me during those weeks of training. I have heard it from many others over the years since. At the time, I reached out to a friend who I admired and trusted. She had many years of experience in the world of foster care and adoption.

"What if a child gets placed with me, and we become too attached, and then they are removed? I know I can't deal with that. It would break my heart!"

Her reply changed my perspective.

"You will get attached. You will get your heart broken when they leave. What you need to remember is it's either your heart that gets broken or theirs."

While her response was hard to digest, it provided clarity. I realized our family unit may never look ideal. We may not have years to pour into someone's life. Then again, we might. We decided that whether it be a lifetime, years, months, days or even just a night, we would be a safe haven for someone who needed it. I was thankful, humbled and a little nervous for the home the Great Architect was designing for us.

Within a few weeks after completing our foster/adoptive classes we received a phone call for a 5-month-old baby girl. Our Dakota. She captured our hearts instantly. Six weeks later... another call. There was a 3-day-old baby girl they wanted to also place with us. Our Addison. Our hearts and arms were full. Seven months later, yet another call. Dakota had a new baby sister. Our Charlie. Such a sweet bundle of love.

A week after our 20th anniversary and just before my 44th birthday, the adoptions were finalized on our three baby girls.... all seven months apart in age!

Life was a crazy kind of beautiful.

Four months later, our youngest daughter Charlie was diagnosed with a rare cancer at 16 months old. Our world was shattered, but we had three pairs of watchful eyes soaking it all in.

We put on happy faces and survived each day on adrenaline and love. During her first two years of treatment, we moved back to Cedar Rapids, Iowa... my husband's hometown.

Because of the curveballs life had thrown, we decided we most likely would never be able foster or adopt again. The proverbial "hands full" statement was an understatement of our daily life.

On the first day of kindergarten for our two oldest girls, I met a sweet little classmate of theirs. She quickly became friends with my girls and found a place in our hearts. She was at our house a lot. Play dates, sleep-overs, and even a spring break trip. I got to know her family pretty well over the years and when they were in a crisis in 2019, they called to see if she could stay with us.

Lily, along with her little brother Gabe, moved in November of 2019... just a few months before Covid rocked our world. During this time, it became apparent that they would need a permanent home. They were already residents of our hearts, so we said yes to them being permanent residents in our home and family.

On a crisp Friday in March 2021, we gathered at Juvenile Court for the official adoption of our Lily and Gabe.

We knew it wouldn't be easy, but is Love supposed to be easy?

Love says yes when self says no.

Love gives when self tries to take.

Love stays when self wants to venture out.

Love is content when self yearns for more.

Some days are reminiscent of many years ago when people told me I had my arms full. I now have a houseful of four teen girls and one pre-teen boy. The coffee and prayers are always flowing!

But every day is also full of purpose, discovery, forgiveness, grace, and chapters still being written in stories that five incredible kids will one day tell.

It's true I am no stranger to heartache.

But now I am also no stranger to Hope.

> ***Come unto me, all you who are weary and burdened, and I will give you rest.***
>
> —Matthew 11:28 KJV

Summary

We all have dreams and ideals in our lives. While we are in the waiting period or even a time of reconstruction, it's so easy to want to make things happen or fix it. Often that doesn't turn out so well. In those tough seasons, try and shift your focus. Find the good during a chaotic day. Laugh when you want to explode. Speak peace when surrounded by life's noise. Cry when you need to, it's okay. If we embrace what we can do, we let the Dream Giver work within us. Beautiful things will begin to unfold... even in the waiting.

2.24

***This is anything but easy, but you are
anything but weak.***

—Unknown

February 24, 2011, is the mark in time that will be
forever etched in my mind. It was the day my sweet,
innocent 12-year-old son received the lifetime diagnosis of Type 1 Diabetes (T1D). T1D is invisible to
most, it is a genetic predisposed autoimmune disorder.
It grips your child's life right along with your own and
it never releases its grip. It is a relentless shadow that
brings a host of emotional stressors that cannot be
adequately articulated with words.

This journey barged into our lives, unwanted and most
definitely undeserved. After all, he was just a kid.

I received a call from the school nurse saying, "Weston isn't feeling well again. You may need to come and pick him up." This happened to be a call that we had already received more than once in a very short span of time and one that was concerning, to say the least.

Clueless as to what could be going on, we scheduled another visit with his pediatrician. Within minutes after arriving we heard him say, "Weston has Type One Diabetes."

With tears in our eyes and hearts that had just been broken into one million pieces, we tried to explain to our son why he had to go the hospital and what was going on.

"But I'm a just a kid. I'll outgrow it," he said.

Oh, how this mama could barely hold it together. My lips quivered and I was biting the inside of my mouth. I wanted to say, "YES of course," but instead I avoided the remark and pretended I didn't hear it. I let his daddy address this one.

I didn't know what all this meant but I did know it was serious.

We were immediately told to get to the children's hospital where we started to learn more. There was so much to digest and take in. I was completely over-whelmed. I remember crying and crying. I didn't know what else to do. I felt as if a part of me had died along with Weston's pancreas.

How was I supposed to say, "No baby, you will not outgrow it and instead you get to deal with this for the rest of your life. You get to poke your fingers to draw blood several times a day. You get to balance your mood, your blood sugar and calculate the carbohydrates on everything you put in your mouth. You get woken up at any point in time in the night so we can check your blood sugar, force you to drink something sugary and then eat so your BS (blood sugar) will stay in range."

We stayed in the Children's Hospital for three days while they monitored him and educated Todd and I, and then Weston was released.

We learned that T1D affects emotions, metabolism, physiology...EVERYTHING! A person living with T1D must think about every morsel of food, every beverage, every illness, and every activity in order to compensate with constant and measured insulin injected doses. It's like having a shadow with you no matter the light conditions. It is in constant pursuit. It never takes a break.

It never goes away.

While February 24, 2011, was the day Weston was diagnosed with Type One Diabetes, a lifelong disease that has changed all our lives forever, it was also the day I began a journey of emotional and spiritual growth that might not have happened otherwise. It was on that day I realized just how small I am and just how much control I do not have. After all, what mama wouldn't try and take the pain, the heartache, the challenge, and the sickness away from your very own child?

We were hurting, yet we found ourselves having the strength to keep moving, one day at a time. And often, one hour at a time. And along the way T1D has taught me so much.

I've learned it's okay to ask God, "Why?" I've learned how to rebuild my faith, I've learned to be tolerant, I've learned to trust even when suffocating in doubt.

Also, on this journey God has proven His faithfulness again and again. I now am humbled to have this blessing and this brokenness in my life. Would I willingly choose this for my son? No! I would take it from him in an instant. But when you place your life in God's hands even the most untenable elements of life have a purpose.

A few years ago, we celebrated his 10-year diagnosis anniversary. I began to reminisce those early days. The days that began not with celebration and joy but with fear, doubt, mourning, guilt, anger, self-pity, and anxiety. All this was so intense and enduring at times that I felt as though I was suffocating. In retrospect my faith in God did not flee, but it was stressed to the brink of collapse.

I prayed and continue to pray for a divine healing wherein the only explanation is the hand of God touching Weston's body. But it hasn't happened... yet.

In the early days after Weston was diagnosed, I found him lying face down on the floor of our family room. Todd asked him, "You okay dude?" As he sat on the floor next to him, he noticed Weston was crying. He asked him again, "What's wrong man?"

Weston said, "Dad, I don't want to do this." He was referring to the procedure of inserting a needle into his belly so he can receive insulin from his pump. (These are the moments when the foreverness of T1D sits atop you with its suffocating weight). As Weston and Todd sat together weeping, I was concerned about his faith in God. I asked if he believed God could heal him and he said yes. It was at this moment my then 13-year-old son uttered these words, "I know it's for a reason."

Today, as I look over my shoulder, I realize and know that God has kept the promise of his word: "Be strong and courageous. Do not be afraid or terrified because of them, for the Lord your God goes with you; he will never leave you nor forsake you." (Deuteronomy 31:6 NIV)

Often, we don't receive our answers from God the moment we ask. We must rely on our faith and push further into life. Then and only then—with experience and wisdom—can we begin to make sense of God's plan.

If I truly believe and have faith in God, then I must mature to the point of accepting that all things not of my doing were prepared for me for a divine and greater purpose. My suffering has a purpose. My suffering has meaning. Suffering renders me humanly helpless; it removes any notion of control I thought I had. It causes me to rely on Him.

Since T1D I can better empathize with people who are afflicted. I can identify with parents whose children are stricken with debilitating disease and other health limitations. My compassion is immediate for people who are afflicted and infirm. Prior to T1D, I was unable to do so with the depth and sincerity I do now.

I am allowing this journey to teach me because I sorely need to be taught. Along this path that God has set me and my family on, I am scouring for wisdom and maturity; not simply for myself but in hoping to help others too.

Now over a decade later, I can testify to the goodness of God for keeping my son safe and healthy.

Weston is an amazingly resilient human being who is not just surviving with Type One Diabetes, but he is THRIVING with Type One Diabetes. I see the hand of God resting upon him as he has dedicated his life to the Kingdom of God. He is strong, he is talented, and he is a witness of God's faithfulness. Weston has not allowed T1D to define who he is, and I know God has planted a ministry in him—a ministry that you can only possess when earned through such an experience.

Using the words of Weston, "I know it's for a reason."

> **Be strong and courageous. Do not be afraid or terrified because of them, for the Lord your God goes with you; he will never leave you nor forsake you.**
>
> —Deuteronomy 31:6 NIV

Summary

Many of life's challenges are not meant to be easy, but they are always meant to teach us, to stretch us, to have us rely on God to be our strength.

2 Corinthians says, "My grace is sufficient for thee: for my strength is made perfect in weakness."

Living with a lifelong diagnosis comes with many fears, many long hard days, and hardships. Only the person diagnosed truly knows how cruel the disease is. BUT the author of our story says we win. The author of our story says he will never leave us nor forsake us. No matter what you may find yourself dealing with, you are never alone, and you WILL be okay. You're an overcomer and your life has an undeniable purpose.

Lean into finding out what that purpose is.

Use it for His glory. Walk in it and never forget what a beautiful gift he has given you.

Faith Of A Child

While we try to teach our children all about life, our children teach us what life is all about.

—Angela Schwindt

It was a sunny winter Monday morning when our 16-month-old daughter Charlie and I made our way to Children's Hospital for some blood work. A week before, a CT scan of her jaw had confirmed that the oral surgeon had been able to fully remove a small cyst on her gum. Because she was tiny, part of her lungs showed up in the image. Lungs viewed on imaging should be mostly black as they are full of air. Hers appeared white and gray, but blurred as this was not the focus of the CT.

This caused the radiologist to call the surgeon, who called our pediatrician, who called us. Whew! He left a voicemail that changed our lives. He said this was a "life altering find" and she needed to see a pediatric pulmonologist at Children's Hospital.

So... back to our Monday morning. After an hour and a half of waiting during what was usually nap time, we were finally called back. Charlie looked over at the empty vials and started crying. I guess she remembered the collapsed vein from a couple of weeks back.

Okay, not a good start.

For the next ten minutes, I sang Elmo's Song, ABC's, Jesus Loves Me... you name it. I was holding this child so tight, and let me tell you, she was fighting.

I glanced over her soft curls to see... nothing. No blood return. Great. Not again.

We moved to the other arm, and the crying, twisting and fighting began again. It was then that a song from years back came to mind, and I started singing in her ear, "I feel Jesus. I feel Jesus. I feel Jesus in this place..."

She melted into my arms.

Still.

Relaxed.

I marveled.

She just laid her head back on me and rested for ten minutes as they continued to draw blood. She rested! Her tears and mine may have intermingled. I sang and she listened. It was a God moment if I have ever had one.

I left that day wishing that I could let every single person who doubts, has been disillusioned, or whose faith is low, that there is a God. His name is Jesus, and that Monday He was felt at a hospital in a small back room of the pediatric lab department.

Everett and I took Charlie back that next Friday for a chest x-ray and to meet with the doctor. Their suspicions were confirmed. There were lesions, spots, holes, and fluid throughout both lungs, and it was urgent that we find out what was causing them. She was admitted for extensive testing. They ran numerous tests, including a Chest CT scan, and put us in isolation for two days.

(They released us just in time, I might add. One morning I found myself eating Starburst jellybeans like popcorn and walking around the room for exercise. Charlie played with her mashed potatoes. We were stir crazy.)

With daily early morning labs, you can imagine the stress level. I watched our sweet girl and was amazed. She was so brave. When they came to draw blood, she would cry and fight the whole time, sometimes screaming, "Mommyyyyy!!"

But as soon as they were done? She would smile, often say a sweet "tank you", and occasionally gave a high five. Then she would always curl up in my lap.

I think when Jesus said in Matthew 19 to "let the children come to him", this is one of the reasons. There is nothing, and I mean nothing like the faith of a child. To be hurt over and over and over, and not hold a grudge.

Still smile.

Still give a high five.

Still search out a lap for security, and arms to hold close when they feel bad.

Now that is faith. That says I trust you. I know you love me. I don't know why this is happening, but I know whose arms I want right now... my mama's or my daddy's.

She ended up needing an open lung biopsy to achieve a diagnosis. As a parent, it broke my heart to see her in pain. But the worry faded because of the look between a mama and her baby girl.

As I peered into Charlie's big beautiful brown eyes, I saw nothing but love and trust. She taught me something that week. No matter what we were about to face, or how much it hurt my heart, I knew where to turn.

I look to the heavens and smile.

I hold no grudges.

God is not my enemy.

His arms are my refuge.

I know He loves me, and He loves Charlie even more than I do.

We had no doubts and nothing to fear. I truly felt that Jesus was walking the hospital halls that week. The rooms were filled with brave little hearts and an undeniable faith so strong. I had no idea what the coming days, weeks, months, and years would hold. But He did. He let me see simple faith in the eyes of my innocent baby girl. I had this feeling He was going to move some pretty big mountains with it!

And the peace of God, which surpasses all understanding, will guard your hearts and your minds in Christ Jesus.

—Philippians 4:7 ESV

Summary

You may not be in a hospital room today, but needing faith is a necessity at any stage in life. For some it's a sickness, for others an important decision needs to be made. Perhaps you have been offered a job or your family is contemplating a big move. Life is full of opportunity, challenges, and new roads, but sometimes the whole leap of faith thing is real. It may not feel like the best thing at that moment but know that God is close by. He is in the room with you. He knows your entire tomorrow before you lay your head on your pillow tonight. Trust Him. Lean on Him. Follow Him. You will be so glad you did.

Sticks, Stones, and Silence

Behind every strong woman is a story that gave her no other choice.

—Nakeia Homer

That moment you can't forget.

That day that seems forever etched in your mind.

The words that you heard.

The text message you read.

The pain you felt.

Rejection.

I think it's safe to say we've all been there. Whether it was a relationship, a job, a promotion, a team, or a friend... the common denominator was the sting.

She was just a young teenager, trying to figure it all out.

She would come home from school in tears and bewilderment as to why her "friends" were so mean to her yet at the same time, so nice to her. The emotional tug-of-war of, "I'm your friend but I am stabbing a knife in your back," seemed to be a reoccurring event and one that broke this mama's heart.

While she wasn't perfect, she didn't deserve this kind of treatment. No one does.

I prayed for her and for God to give me wisdom and the correct words to help my sweet girl.

I would wipe the tears from her eyes and tell her how much I loved her, and how that Jesus loved her even more.

I encouraged her to pray for her enemies, and to be a bright light in this dark world.

Hurting people, hurt people.

While she was hurting, I prayed that God would heal the shattered pieces of her heart.

I watched her grow into a beautiful, confident, and mature young woman, who could have returned the treatment she had been given, but instead chose to rise above. But God.

There are moments in life that you can't begin to comprehend or make sense of.

Often it is compounded by the lack of communication. You try and replay scenarios in your mind. You second guess. You self-criticize. You internalize. You sabotage your joy because of the perception and actions of another.

I'll be the first to admit that there have been times when I didn't navigate dismissive waters very well. I was frantically flailing and attempting to shout above the roar of my crashing self-esteem.

Words matter.

Words kill and destroy.

Words can lift one up and give the hearing ears the wings to fly.

Not only do the words you say to others influence their life, but the words you say to yourself are equally as important.

Daily affirmations are the nourishment our minds need to thrive and grow. Positive words can help boost our self-confidence, improve our mental well-being, and cultivate a positive mindset.

Several years ago, I started making it a habit of speaking kind and empowering words to myself every day.

Cultivating compassionate self-talk takes practice, but its benefits are transformative. It boosts confidence, reduces stress, and fosters resilience. Your words have the power to shape your reality, so let them be a source of love and encouragement. After all, you are fearfully and wonderfully made and there is no one else in the world who is exactly like you.

Who you are and what you have to offer is necessary and valuable.

There's no point in comparing yourself or your journey to others because no one can do what you do, exactly how you do it.

Oh, what a beautiful soul you are. You are royalty, you are a child of the King and you are created in HIS image.

So, what is one to do when left with unanswered questions of the heart?

How do you heal the brokenness and somehow just move on?

You just keep walking.

Keep moving.

Keep reaching.

Keep smiling.

Keep doing.

Keep loving.

When you want to retreat, schedule a lunch.

When you want to disappear, wear the red dress.

When you want to settle, shout your dreams from the rooftops.

When you want to circle the wagons, whisper a prayer for those who hurt you.

When you want to push others away, initiate the hug.

Life is full of beautiful days and celebrations, heartaches and starting over.

You are strong, capable, worthy, and full of potential.

You are unique and you are chosen.

Remember that.

You can carry the rock of bitterness with you through life, or you can give it to God.

Being a victim of bullying most certainly leaves you scarred for life. I'm so thankful to say that while this period in my daughter's life could have had adverse effects, now ten years later, I see more than ever that Jesus used it for her good. He gave her the gentlest, kindest, most forgiving, loving, serving, and passionate heart. I see such beauty in the ashes, beauty in the scar.

Get rid of all bitterness, rage and anger, brawling and slander, along with every form of malice. Be kind and compassionate to one another, forgiving each other, just as in Christ God forgave you.

—Ephesians 4:31-32 NIV

Summary

We live in a broken world, so it's natural and part of this thing called life to have that brokenness bleed over into our relationships. As we read, God's word is clear that we need to try to rid ourselves of the poison that bitterness, anger, and resentment cause. But it isn't always easy. A perfectly healed friendship or relationship takes time, patience, and effort from both parties. In the meantime, just start with doing one thing each day. Choose to be kind. Choose to forgive. Choose to love.

Capturing Courage

Sometimes it's the scars that remind you that you survived. Sometimes the scars tell you that you have healed.

—Ashley D. Wallis

It was a unique moment in time. A few days earlier, the world as we had known it had collided with a world that felt so foreign. At first, I thought we were intruders. A wrong turn had dropped us here. Perhaps it was a dream and morning would soon come to jolt me back to reality.

The fresh scar over her left rib cage taunted me. What we thought was a touch of pneumonia was instead numerous lesions filling both lungs. Her oncologist said they stopped counting after 75. They suspected it was in her bone marrow.

Shaken.

Broken.

Tired.

Scared.

Determined.

We found a photographer and set a date. I quieted my mind while walking through Children's Place and Old Navy. A friend found the perfect little outfit and handed it to me in a Chick-fil-a parking lot. The church kids made her a bracelet that said "courage".

Numb.

Forgetful.

Breathless.

It was a windy but beautiful day in early Spring. A train rumbled through and my oldest buried her head in my shoulder. Tears were wiped away. Smiles were present. Laughter was heard. Hugs were plentiful. The sound of the shutter bringing comfort that this day, this time, this moment would be remembered.

You may be in a moment of unknown.

Perhaps bad news was in your last phone call or text.

Perhaps your job is uncertain.

Perhaps you found out you will need to relocate.

Perhaps your home is too quiet.

While the road ahead may seem daunting and unsure, I hope you find a reason to laugh.

To wipe a tear away. To yell over the blaring of a train. To make memories.

Because I promise you...

One day you will look back from the other side of the unknown and you will draw strength from how far you have come.

Resilient.

Fearless.

Courageous.

You won't recall when those words became a part of your life. Were they always there?

A black and white photo draws you in and then... you see it.

It was in their little innocent eyes that day.

Childlike faith.

Trust.

Hope.

You are at peace and assured you can face any of tomorrow's unknowns.

If your heart is broken, you'll find God right there; if you're kicked in the gut, he'll help you catch your breath.

—Psalm 34:18 MSG

Summary

Someone once said that if you aren't going through something now, it's because you just got out of it or it's just around the corner. Maybe a big life tragedy hasn't knocked at your door, but one thing is for sure. Your pain is your pain. Your grief or loss, regardless of magnitude and without comparison, is real. If you are feeling disappointment or hurt in any way, take comfort that you are not alone. Your Creator is ever present. There are other humans who have walked on broken paths. You are not alone.

The Hotdog

The mind replays what the heart can't forget.

—Unknown

She was shy to the core.

A tiny little thing at only nine years of age.

One day stands out in her mind, some forty-four years later. This day has had an impact on her life in more ways than one.

It started out like any other ordinary day for this third grader. She got out of bed, got dressed, ate breakfast, and reluctantly left for school. School was not her favorite place to be.

Fast forward to the noon lunch break and the one thing she looked forward to every day. She sat at a table in the cafeteria with all her little friends. They giggled and talked as they ate the lunch food that was on the menu for that day.

Unbeknown to this little girl, the rule at this school at this time was that you had to eat ALL the food that you were given. I'm sure this rule no longer exists but at the time, this was how it was. Normally, she took her lunch, which usually consisted of a peanut butter sandwich, Chef Boyardee Spaghetti O's and meatballs—remember those? so gross—and vanilla pudding or applesauce.

That day she decided to try what was on the lunch menu, not realizing until after the fact that what she'd be given was something she disliked very much.

Well, she HATED it.

Hotdogs.

She had only eaten a hotdog once in her short lifetime and she wasn't about to eat another one, not on this day or any other day for that matter.

As the allotted lunch break was winding down, one by one her friends were allowed to get up, clear off their trays and proceed outside for the much anticipated and best part of the day, recess.

She looked around and found that she was the only child still in the cafeteria. Being the timid child she was, she just sat there in silence and all alone.

FINALLY, an adult monitoring the cafeteria approached her and asked her if she was ready to go outside and play. Of course, she quietly replied with a nod, instead of a hearty and bold yes. She started to get up from where she had been sitting and suddenly, she was told by the adult to sit back down. The little girl did as she was told yet very confused and frightened. "What? Why can't I go outside and play with my friends?"

Then it happened.

Words that stuck with her for a very long time. Words that stung and pierced her heart like a fiery dart. To most, these words would not have made a profound impact, but to this child on this day, they did.

"You are in trouble. You've not followed the rules. You will be punished. You see child, you have to eat your hotdog before you can go outside." The harsh words and the tone in which they were spoken, broke her little heart. You see, she had never heard words spoken "like this" in her nine years of life. She hated hotdogs, and the thoughts of feeling like she was going to be made to eat one was too much for her to bear.

There was no stopping the tears that began to swell up in her eyes and roll down her cheeks.

She couldn't eat the hotdog, which also meant she couldn't go outside and play with her friends.

What felt like the longest lunch break in the world eventually timed out, and all students returned to class.

A few hours passed and the time came when she was able to burst through the door of where she found love, comfort, care, and understanding. She was home and was eager to share what had happened that cruel day, with her parents.

The following day her father was not about to allow what happened the previous day go unnoticed. The words he had with the school principal basically ensured that his daughter could go to school and would not be forced to eat food she didn't like or want to eat and would not be punished for it ever again.

Thankfully, that day never repeated itself again. (Thanks, Dad.)

Why would I choose to tell you this story about The Hotdog?

Some would say, "It's just a hot dog, for goodness sake." Others might question, "Is this story significant enough to write about it in a ladies' devotional? After all, what's the big deal?"

Yes, it's significant and this is the reason why.

Allow me to share a little more about this little girl for you to get the bigger picture and the why behind me sharing The Hotdog story with you.

This little girl was me.

I remember it like it was yesterday.

I felt like I had done something horribly wrong.

I felt so ashamed.

I felt like a loser.

I felt stupid, after all, it was just a hotdog.

I felt all alone.

I was confused.

I was hurt.

I felt abandoned.

I felt bullied and picked on.

I felt as if my heart had been crushed by a trusted adult.

I was already shy, timid, and scared of my own shadow. The Hotdog, while it was just an incident that took place within a short lunch period that felt like eternity, for some reason had a lasting impact that I carried with me for a very long time. For several weeks, months, and even years, I was fearful of other adults. I hid behind my parents and siblings. I became even more of an introvert and really didn't emerge outside this cozy comfort zone until adulthood when I was forced to communicate and build adult relationships. I was most definitely on the struggle bus and felt years behind in this area of my life.

While the words only took seconds to cut my heart, the effect on my emotional well-being had an impact for many years to come, as you can see.

Maybe you don't have a hot dog story, but maybe you've been spoken to in a way that left you feeling hurt, scared, or embarrassed. Perhaps you've been told you don't matter, your voice isn't important, or you aren't smart enough. Maybe you've been mistreated by peers, an adult (like I was), or even a parent. Maybe your scar was self-inflicted by the thoughts or words you've told yourself.

Maybe you were the person who at one time or another spoke unkind words to others. Maybe a hurtful circumstance caused you to inflict hurt on another.

Words matter.

They either build up or tear down. They either lift others up or knock them to their knees.

Words are life and death.

Words are powerful.

"Sticks and stones will break my bones, but words will never hurt me." WRONG!

Words DO hurt.

Words DO break us.

Words DO leave scars.

There came a time that I had to let the wound heal. I stopped picking at the scab and making it bleed over and over again. Now when I look back on those early tender years, I remember the hurt but the scar itself has faded with time. I think because of that pain, I now have an increased intuition to others who are facing wounds of the heart.

You too will be able to turn the hurt into something that can help others. Your story, regardless of how silly (hotdogs), how big or small, how significant or not, needs to be shared. There is something good that can emerge from the deep and ugly wound.

Kind words heal and help; cutting words wound and maim.

—Proverbs 15:4 MSG

Summary

If you find yourself thinking back on old wounds, allow the mending and healing to begin. God will be there to swoop you up in his loving arms and hold you. You will be all right. Don't carry this hurt with you. Forgive and let it go. He wants to heal you, but you first must be ready. Give Him all your brokenness, hurt, and pain. Sweet friend, I pray you find a place of healing and when you see that scar that it serves as a reminder of all you have conquered, and you find blessing and grace for each day.

Letting Them Walk

There really are places in the heart you don't even know exist until you love a child.

—Ann Lamont

I wasn't prepared for this. I have seen those words or even said them myself since becoming a parent. I wasn't prepared for this. Often that phrase is used in describing things like lack of sleep, endless laundry, cooking dinner with one on a hip and one grabbing your ankle, showering at 8:35 pm because they are finally off to slumber...

All of that is real and exhausting, but I have found just over the past year, there is something much deeper that I wasn't prepared for.

You don't see a lot of writings about it because to be quite honest, it's not an easy read. There aren't three easy steps to frame the words that just flowed from a weary heart.

I wasn't prepared to love this much. The knot in the throat kind of love. To see absolute greatness in the innocent eyes that trust you completely yet also see little shoulders that slump. Lips that quiver. Voices that soften to a whisper to share what their tiny heart is screaming.

Some have called it tough love. It's tough because we realize these little people are learning life by doing. How I would love to make each day of my kids' lives rainbows and unicorns, but they are walking the path that we all are walking. They have seasons where their feet are unsteady. It would be so easy for me to reach out, scoop them up in my arms, and say, "Let me do that."

But we let them walk this walk called childhood. They laugh. They cry. They get scared. They squeal with delight. They make mistakes. They excel. They love. They get angry. They forgive. They snuggle close. They play.

Then when they lay their head on their pillow to rest, we scoop them up in our arms. We pray words of life and purpose and potential and kindness over them. We ask the angels to protect them. We whisper that they are perfect and exactly what God designed them to be.

I wasn't prepared for this, but I was hand-picked by the Great Creator for this. To be this mom to these wee ones. In this moment.

You were handpicked, my friend. If life is swallowing you up right now, bills are piling up, teens are giving the silent treatment, or babies are up all night... always remember this. You may not feel adequately prepared but take great assurance that you are loved and watched and followed closely by our Heavenly Father who is letting you walk it out.

Tonight, when all is quiet and you lay your head on your pillow to rest, I hope you hear His whisper that says, "You are perfect and exactly what I designed you to be."

The LORD your God is in your midst,
a mighty one who will save; he will
rejoice over you with gladness; he will
quiet you by his love; he will exult
over you with loud singing.

—Zephaniah 3:17 ESV

Summary

Whether you are a parent or not, you may still relate. Is there a friend or loved one that is in difficult or unfamiliar territory? It's tempting to want to take over, but you know deep inside that you can't. This is something they must walk through. What you can do is love them through it. Be present. Let them know you are close by. Encourage them. Pray for them. Perhaps you are trudging through the unknown. Your heavenly Father has gone before you and He has promised to never leave you alone. One foot in front of the other, my friend. You've got this.

On Her Knees

To nurture a garden is to feed not just the body, but the soul.

—Unknown

The sun is shining, and warmer temperatures have arrived.

There she goes again, spade in hand and a smile on her face that couldn't be wiped off if you had to.

She likes the feel of soil running through her fingers and her hands, so she doesn't bother with putting on her garden gloves.

She's bent over, she's on her knees, she's in her happy place.

My mom has grand plans each summer and anticipates the blooms in her growing flower beds.

She works from sunup to sundown during those first few weeks of the new season. Who am I kidding? She works like that all summer long and even well into the fall.

Before long all the planting, pruning, moving, plucking, weeding, and watering pays off. The garden master has tenderly and lovingly groomed some of the most gorgeous flowers that in return, bloom for her all season long.

On her knees, she not only tends to her passion, but she also tends to her purpose.

She has cultivated a lifestyle of prayer.

Her prayers as a wife, a mother, a grandmother, and a friend are priceless. Her prayers are a gem, a rare treasure.

The vase on her dining room table, a breathtaking display of blooms she handpicks on any given day.

Each flower serves as a reminder of seeds planted and the nurturing that has taken place.

Each prayer is like a seed, dropped in the soil of Heaven.

These flowers are a representation of the lives her prayers have touched.

The prayers of protection when she knows a family member is traveling.

The prayers prayed for her family's ambitions, careers, and endeavors.

The prayers of salvation for a dear friend, healing for the hurting neighbor, peace for those in turmoil, direction for the wandering, and strength for weak.

The number of prayers she has prayed, only God knows. What I do know is that God heard those prayers, He answered those prayers, He listened, and He cared.

Each prayer is still touching the ears of Heaven like the dirt touching her fingertips. The seeds that she planted have and will continue to grow deep into the soil of life. The weeds she plucks out to ensure her children and their children's children have the blessings and favor of God upon their lives. Mom has sown seeds of faith, trust, and biblical truths so deep they can't help but take root.

It doesn't always look pretty and often her gardening comes with pain.

Her back aches from the constant bending over, the digging, the hauling and even the moving of rocks to form a barrier of safety for her plants.

Her knees are dirty and might need a little extra soaking in her bath at night.

There are times her fingers are pricked by the ugly unforeseen thorns.

There are times she cannot save the dying plant, but often, through the proper light and love, there is a flourishing flower in no time.

For Mom's flower gardens to look their best requires a tremendous amount of grace, patience, and energy.

Her work isn't in vain.

Her prayer investments pay off.

Oh, to be like Mom.

It's no secret that I've killed more than one plant in my days. Mom has been my flower doctor for years and would tell me when the soil was too dry, too wet, exposed to too much sun or not enough. Somehow, she always knows just what the pathetic looking flower needs and would have it thriving and back home to me in no time. But not before reminding me first of the proper care this plant would need to keep growing and live a healthy life.

What happens when we forget to pray, and push the Bible to the wayside? We become unhealthy. We are exposed to the elements of this world and then we are left fighting a battle that was never intended for us to fight alone. We become parched. Without prayer and the word of God our spiritual lives are threatened with pests and diseases. We are exposed to hail, heat, and damaging winds.

Although Mom spends time with God through prayer and devotion every morning, it doesn't stop there, instead she carries them with her throughout the days which have made up her entire life. It's the very essence of her being. She doesn't miss a day, a moment, or opportunity to tend to her prayer garden.

Several years ago, I decided it was necessary for me to dedicate a specific time each day to spend in prayer, just like Mom.

It was time for me to begin cultivating my own prayer life.

It took me months and even years to find a good rhythm. Each day, I had the choice of getting up and praying or going about my day without it.

It wasn't easy, but I persevered.

And through it I learned a valuable secret: Our daily choices matter.

To get up every day and just spend a few minutes in prayer and devotion has transformed my life and therefore the life of generations to come.

I see with each passing day the seeds that were sown by mom; the cultivating, the nourishing, the watering, and the tender love and care are producing the most beautiful flowers. The harvest is plenty. The roots are deep.

The most treasured and valuable lesson she ever taught me... was on her knees.

And that Christ will live in your hearts because of your faith. Stand firm and be deeply rooted in his love.

—Ephesians 3:17 CEV

Summary

Don't let the busyness of life keep you from praying and studying God's word. Stay soaked in His presence, absorbing every ounce of love and wisdom. Not only that, but we are to put what we read into practice. Growing every day to become more and more like Him. Learning from our experiences and increasing our faith.

Unfortunately, we let our minds, our thoughts, or dreams and our days get overrun with weeds and we fail to water during the drier days. During the seasons of drought and darkness, we sit dormant instead of getting on our knees.

Just like cultivating a flower garden takes effort and dedication, so does cultivating a prayer life. If we neglect prayer, we tend to find our lives barren and empty.

A growing prayer life can't blossom without a little work.

Do the work, do it consistently, do it intentionally and watch your life begin to blossom.

My Sister

Through scars the ministry will unfold.

—Unknown

A preacher's daughter.

A Christian school graduate.

A mama, a daughter, a wife, and my sister.

Church was our life. Attending youth conventions, camps, and multiple services per week, she was basically raised on the church pew.

She was drawn to Jesus at the tender age of 6. By the time she was 8, she was fully committed to Him.

She was a good person and came from a pretty great family, if I say so myself!

She was called to the serve in ministry at the age of 15.

Shortly after graduating from high school, she married her first love who also happened to be in ministry. Together they worked in various positions as youth pastors, assistant pastor, and church planters. They started not one but two Christian schools. This was all she had known. She was truly born for this. Life was great.

Or was it?

I remember the day she told me the heartbreaking news that shattered the world we knew. The news that shattered our family. The news that broke the heart of my sweet sister. After 16 years of marriage, she shared that her husband told her he was living a double life.

She was devastated.

She was hurt, embarrassed, broken; and even though she had done nothing wrong, she felt ashamed. She felt as if her entire life had been a lie. She began to doubt God and His word. Because of shame and confusion, she withdrew and became isolated from the very ones who could help her through this horrific storm.

She began to believe the lies of the enemy. The ones that said, "Who are you now?"

You're no longer a preacher's wife.

You're a failure.

You're damaged.

You're a reject.

You can never minister again... that life is over.

She lost her identity. She lost touch with her purpose. Not wanting to face the hurt and confusion, she ran. She ran away from God and family. She ran far away from the only world she had known and the ones who loved her most.

Three months after the divorce, she met and married a man who, unbeknownst to her, was an abusive alcoholic. I remember her calling to tell me that she was getting married, and I begged her not to. For her to be able to think reasonably was not in her emotional nor mental capacity.

Soon the bad became horrible. She went down a very dark path. She lost her song. She stepped into a cultish religion that was foreign to her, but she somehow thought it would bring her peace of mind.

Unfortunately, this move did quite the opposite.

The next four years she found herself fighting for her life. She tells of the lonely, miserable nights, the bruises and blood, the tear-filled pillow, the silent screams of, "This isn't me. This isn't me. I want out. I want out!" There were a few times she would walk out and in no time found herself walking right back into that foreign land. Our family didn't see her very often and when we did, it gave us a short-lived sense of peace, just to know she was alive and breathing. We certainly questioned the fake smile and happiness she so desperately tried to convey. We knew better.

She was estranged from family and friends and found herself lonely and afraid. She vividly remembers the night she decided she could not stay any longer. She had just been thrown to the floor and began to bleed, and for a moment she thought she was losing her baby. Speaking of her baby, I questioned why God could give her a child under these circumstances and was so upset when we received the news.

But He had a much bigger plan.

God heard her cry. You see, she didn't have the strength to leave on her own. She didn't think she deserved it. So He sent along a tiny little baby, my beautiful niece. She only weighed three pounds and thirteen ounces, but she saved Jennifer's life. Jennifer did not want to raise her baby in this world she'd come to know.

At this time in her life, she knew she needed to get back home. She longed for the comfort and safety she knew was waiting for her.

She returned home with a little bundle of joy attached. HOME never looked so good.

Three weeks later, on a Sunday morning, she slipped onto the back pew of her daddy's church; and there she sat—broken, empty and dead inside. Emotionally, physically, spiritually, and mentally depleted! She gave all the broken pieces to God that day, August 9th, 2010, and God showed up.

God had a different plan for Jennifer's life.

That was over 10 years ago.

Everything the devil stole from my sister, everything she walked away from... God has restored. We never stopped praying that God would bring her back home. We never lost hope, we never gave up on God. She has remarried and is in active ministry today. It's so beautiful to witness Jennifer bringing hope to those who are still out there longing and searching for a better way and are crying out for help.

She found her TRUE identity and purpose.

There IS purpose after brokenness and beauty in ashes. My sister is living proof that God is faithful. He will never leave you nor forsake you.

What a miracle, a testimony of grace, redemption, and restoration.

Look what God did.

Look what God is still doing.

*For I know the plans I have for you,
declares the Lord, plans to prosper
you and not to harm you, plans to give
you hope and a future.*

—Jeremiah 29:11 NIV

Summary

Have you ever felt so lost, confused, defeated, and hurt that you couldn't see your way out? Has the hurt caused you to run to the world instead of Jesus?

He's waiting for you with open arms to return to the fold. Jesus is ready to pick you up right where you are. He loves you in your brokenness. He is in your mess. Run to the Father and find hope, peace, forgiveness and restoration.

He is there!

Change

When the winds of change blow, some people build walls and others build windmills.

—Unknown

Today, one of my littles walked in the house and I saw it. Her eyes. They spoke words her lips would not form.

I have seen that look before... in a stranger's eyes, a new coworker's eyes, and even my own as the mirror dared just a passing glance.

Change. A simple word with so many complexities.

It is often wrapped in beautiful papers, words scripted on the finest parchment, and the bow meticulously looped and tied with care. But with the precious gift of change there are usually moments, days, and for some... long seasons of wistfulness and reflection.

I called it a gift because of my own frame of reference. I will be the first to proclaim that I do NOT covet change! Quite the contrary. There is true comfort in using the same coffee cup each day, sitting in the same chair, with the same blanket, and quietly contemplating life, reading the words of the One who loves me and triple checking my calendar. Yet, I have found the gift of change has brought new friendships, strengthened old ones, stretched me out of my comfort zone, and opened unexpected doors.

Back to my little munchkin. We had recently moved to a new house. The girls were part of the house hunting process all along and they were so excited and filled with anticipation. The first couple of nights, they stayed up way too late. Full of giggles and silliness. They adored their new rooms, loved riding bikes in the cul-de-sac and thoroughly enjoyed playing with some of their classmates and new friends in the neighborhood. We met many of our neighbors and had felt welcomed.

Yet this night, she missed the familiar. The backyard gate she knew she could walk through at any time, the little friend who was always ready to play, the boundaries she had been used to, the friend who was like a big sister, the lights and sounds of the house she'd known since a toddler.

I saw the look. We talked. We laughed. We hugged. I reassured her that those things were not lost, just different.

She took a deep breath and jumped up to play some more. What teachers these sweet girls are to me.

I sat in the dark quiet of my new living room for a long time after they were all sound asleep. I wondered about all the many people who, even tonight, saw the look in a mirror as they walked by. I prayed they knew that what they had was not lost. It may have been different, but not lost.

Change. There will be good days and not so good days, but God can and WILL fill you with all joy and peace. And one day very soon... the new of today will be the comfort and familiar of yesterday.

***The God of hope fill you with all joy
and peace.***

—Romans 15:13 NIV

Summary

Oh, how the thought of change carries so much emotion for some. It's something that most of us have experienced once or twice or too many times to count. Some welcome it while others try to avoid it at all costs.

We may live in a state of confusion over a seemingly positive change, all because life happened. Don't let second guessing get the best of you in those times. Romans 8:28 is a reminder that He works all things together for His good. Ask the Lord for peace during a time of painful transition. Relish in the blessings of new adventures. There truly is hope and joy for all of life's seasons.

Broken but Chosen

It is in your broken places you are most often used by God.

—Christine Caine

I never imagined this, but He called me here. I want to run to the beauty that beckons, yet a reflection in the mirror causes me to stay. The lines on my face tell a story. Our story.

The story hasn't been pretty lately. All kinds of adjustments being made by parents who are just plain tired and by kids who are carrying wounds of the heart. Voices have risen.

Expectations not met.

Disappointment in one another and in ourselves.

Yet the call was so clear.

So then how did we get here?

To this moment.

To this place of perceived defeat.

The pain in my eyes fades when I hear a soft voice.

"Mommy?"

My smile is from ear to ear. Matching hers. The gift God sent as a living breathing balm to wounds no eye can see. As chatter and laughter from the young ones lift Heavenward, I sense peace descending. Calm fills the hallways and rooms of this place we call home. The ebb and flow of tension and pure joy are a testament to grace for each day.

Maybe you have found yourself in a place most unexpected. Perhaps the clouds are swirling overhead, just daring you to take that first step. Do you lie awake at night, heart racing? You may feel a combination of dreams and doubts troubling once still waters.

Breathe in. Breathe out. Repeat.

You are in His exceptional care.

You are on His mind.

You are part of His plans.

You are remembered.

You are watched over.

The Good Book says that although we can't see (understand) it all clearly at the present... we are promised a day when clarity will come.

I imagine we will behold in reverent silence our every pain, every hurt, every question, every scar, and every fragile piece of our heart.

It will be stunning.

Then the voice that called us to broken pathways and unknown places will gently say our name. In one sacred redemptive moment we will have clarity. It will be so worth it. Carry on, my friend. You are wildly loved, protected, overflowing with strength and never ever alone.

> *Let us not become weary in doing good, for at the proper time we will reap a harvest if we do not give up.*

—Galatians 6:9 NIV

Summary

We all have something inside that motivates us to face each day. Whether it is with joy and excitement or weariness and tears, it is the thing that governs our days. Others may glance our way with raised eyebrows or question our sanity or motives. Only you know the entirety of your heart. You don't need to explain it to everyone. Keep on the path He brought you to. Trust your gut. Trust your God.

When There Are No Blossoms

Every season is one of becoming, but not always one of blooming. Be gracious with your ever evolving self.

—B. Oakman

I love mornings. Really. The birds chatting with each other, sounds of a tired city just waking, a gentle and slightly cool breeze.

A quiet house.

Okay, so now you know the real reason I like mornings. :-)

This morning, I stepped outside for just a minute and was admiring many beautiful flowers, plants, and trees along our street. The aroma was divine. Then I looked at my sad rose bush and two other plants of unknown origin and made a mental note to get a green thumb over here to help a girl out!

The past few weeks have been a lesson in faith and patience. Some things trivial but constant, while other things are potentially life changing. I have always felt that when going through tough times the Lord wants me to rest, trust, hope, receive, extend grace, and just keep walking.

I have had the opportunity to meet some amazing people over the past few years who have done just that. Their roots went deep, their tears watered the dry ground, their situation was covered in God's love, and yet they waited. For just a blossom. A sprig of hope. A blade of green.

A few weeks after we first received the news of Charlie's diagnosis, the results came in that it was also in her bone marrow. I remember crying in a parking lot and texting a few people with the news. A mom whose child had the same disease replied with this scripture:

Even though the fig trees have no blossoms, and there are no grapes on the vine; even though the olive crop fails, and the fields lie empty and barren; even though the flocks die in the fields, and the cattle bans are empty, yet I will rejoice in the LORD! I will be joyful in the God of my salvation. –Habakkuk 3:17-18 NLT

This was the sprig of hope I needed. Just rejoice...

Rejoice when you are worried.

Rejoice when you just received bad news.

Rejoice when the heavens are silent.

Rejoice when your heart feels like it's been stepped on.

Rejoice when the miracle is elusive.

Rejoice when words have hurt.

Rejoice as you pack up your things due to company downsizing. Rejoice while you wait. Rejoice when the answer is far from what you had expected. I wish I had answers for the many questions of life.

I don't understand the why's, but I know the One who does.

I know that rejoicing in Him, even if it's accompanied with many shouts and tears, is nurturing the soil of my heart.

My friend, He is tending to you.

He steps out and checks on you each morning.

He carefully prunes.

He knows about the drought.

He sends rain to your soul.

He sees beauty.

He sees a garden full of life and green.

He loves His time with you.

He loves caring for you. Really.

> *To appoint unto them that mourn in Zion, to give unto them beauty for ashes, the oil of joy for mourning, the garment of praise for the spirit of heaviness; that they might be called trees of righteousness, the planting of the LORD, that he might be glorified.*
>
> —Isaiah 61:3 KJV

Summary

Life has a way of deterring some of our biggest plans and goals. Sometimes we have a big hand in it and other times we are left to wonder if we are doing something wrong or maybe dreamed too big. If you have something on your heart and you wonder if it will happen, take heart in knowing that God is watching over you. He alone knows everything about you, including that dream that you keep coming back to. His timing is impeccable. Stay deeply rooted in Him, whether you see a blossom or not.

But For a Moment

The most painful goodbyes are the ones that are never said and never explained.

—Unknown

The telephone rang.

I answered it with a typical happy, "Hello?"

On the other end was an unfamiliar voice and one I was trying hard to place. Who could this be?

The sweet introduced herself, and within minutes, I felt like I had known her for years. You know, those relationships that come out of nowhere and form overnight?

We talked for forty-five minutes.

Obviously, we connected from the get-go. That was the start of a friendship that I wasn't necessarily looking for at the time but embraced it and ran with it. From that day forward we were practically inseparable. We had so much in common it was kind of creepy.

For example, on many occasions we would find ourselves finishing one another's thoughts and sentences. We spent long hours that ran into days, weeks, months, and even years. We even braved a family vacation and a few camping trips together.

One of the fondest memories I have is how we loved to laugh together. We would often make one another even snort laugh. I'm sure you know what kind of laugh that is?

But more than the laughs, Helen and I shared many tears and heartaches. We shared past experiences, pain, and failures. I was able to give her words of encouragement without judgement. I was able to bring her hope and a closer look into a relationship with Jesus.

Helen was by my side and a companion to me when I had lost my dearest and most precious sidekick. My built-in best friend, my sister. I had not lost my sister in death but in a religious cult that suddenly tore her away from my family. Death while living is how I saw it.

While Helen didn't replace my sister of course, she sure filled the gaping cavity down deep in my breaking heart.

Helen was also the one that I called immediately when our family was given the most horrific news and was enroute to Riley Children's Hospital. We were just given Weston's Type One Diabetes diagnosis. Helen consoled me and even cried with me. Being the kind-hearted friend she had become, Helen didn't hesitate to shower our family with never-ending love and support, on that horrible day and for many months and years to follow. This source of strength was more than comforting and medicine for our souls.

I remember thinking how on earth had I gone through life thus far without a beautiful friendship like this. We seemed to just get each other in so many ways and on so many levels. I remember thinking this kind of friendship would last forever, or would it?

It took me several years to figure out WHY. Why had God blessed me with such a strong bond and sisterhood like no other?

Why was this friendship SO strong for a few years, yet so weak it broke apart in seconds?

It wasn't for several years after our friendship had ended that God dropped into my wondering mind one day the why!

I finally got it.

It was a friendship that was only to be temporary.

It was a friendship that wasn't to be long term.

Helen was meant to be in my life to be a companion for the journey I was on at that time.

I was gently reminded by my Heavenly Father that I had not done anything wrong.

It was not about me, but instead it was more about Him.

He was showing me that He was faithful and is ALWAYS looking out for me.

He blessed me with Helen when I didn't even realize that I needed a Helen kind of friendship.

For a reason, for a season, or for a lifetime?

All I know is God knew, and that's all that matters.

If you find yourself with a broken friendship, a sister-hood bond that crumbled without a day's notice or a relationship that was torn apart for various reasons, be at peace knowing that perhaps it was meant to be that way.

Perhaps you have or will have a Helen in your life.

Love her.

Enjoy her.

Smile with memories of times shared together.

Your friendship had meaning and purpose.

May you always remember that.

> ***To every thing there is a season, and a time to every purpose under the heaven.***

> —Ecclesiastes 3:1 KJV

Summary

Don't be afraid to go in a different direction and allow friendships to take their natural course. After all, friendship breakups are also a normal part of life. It can be natural for a friendship to end when a job ends, or you move to a new city. It's not uncommon to outgrow friendships either and this doesn't mean someone has to take the blame or that you did something wrong. Letting go can feel really hard in these situations, but hanging on to what isn't meant to be is even harder in the long run. Trust God with these broken relationships, pray for them and allow mending and a healing to take place if that is meant to be. At the same time, understand and be accepting that sometimes God allows there to be a separation and a parting of ways, all for the greater good.

Six Weeks and a Day

May the flowers remind us why the rain was so necessary.

—Xan Oku

The night was just beginning, and it was cruel. Bad news had just been given to my family, and just a few hours later I was supposed to fall asleep as if it was any ordinary night? Yeah right.

But let me share how the evening started out for a second.

I'll never forget the phone ringing, me answering, as I was awaiting a test result, and hearing, "You have cancer."

What?

No way?

How is this possible?

They must have the wrong number?

The next few hours were a blur but a few things I do remember more than I'd like to.

As the earth-shattering news began to settle in my mind, so did reality. The reality was Cancer had now hit our family. Cancer could change my life forever. Cancer could take me from this earth. Cancer could dominate and rule what life I MIGHT have left.

I began to question it all.

Was there a mix up in the files?

Did they mean to call someone else, not me?

Were the findings accurate?

Was I going to die from this horrible disease?

Would I have to endure months of cruel treatment?

What now?

Why?

I asked why.

I asked God why would He allow something like this to happen to me in the prime of my life?

How do I tell the kids?

Oh, this was a big one. I cried and cried. My husband held me. I cried some more and while shaking and shattered I told him, "I don't want the kids to know, I don't want them to worry." Now you must understand my children at the time were not littles. Our daughter was twenty-three and our son was twenty. So, one could say, our children were young adults. This mama just likes to call her offspring children instead of adults.

Makes me not sound quite as old, right?

So we did the hard.

We told them the bad news.

We prayed together as a family and then it was bedtime.

In the dark, in the stillness, in the quiet, fear began to grip my mind.

Fear began to wedge its way in whether I wanted it to or not.

Anxiety was attempting to set up camp and the air in my lungs was sucked out of me. It was hard to even breathe.

BUT then the most beautiful thing happened.

My husband Todd and I began to usher in the holy presence of the Healer himself. As we were letting the words "you have cancer" soak in, we also fell to our knees and cried out to our Savior.

What else could we do?

I'll never forget how HE showed up. In a still small voice, He spoke to us. He began to calm our storm. In an instant peace fell into our bedroom, into our hearts and into these new uncharted waters. I had never experienced this kind of peace before. This kind of peace felt like a soft, warm, cozy blanket. I wrapped myself in it. I clung to it for the next six weeks and didn't let go.

He was oh so VERY present from then on. He spoke to us in a clear and audible voice. His word pierced our hearts as he reminded us to "Be STILL and KNOW I am God."

Over the next six weeks, I saw God move in ways I could have never imagined. From directing us to the best surgeon many miles from home to my story being shared on a stage in front of 15,000 people.

A ministry was born on this day. Like all births it was painful, it was hard, it was scary, it was messy, it was oh so beautiful.

We got the news just one week after surgery that all was clear. The cancer was gone, and no further treatment needed. Oh, what an answered prayer that was. We rejoiced. We celebrated. We thanked the Lord for hearing our cries and for being so faithful.

BE STILL... shhhh, hush, be quiet, stop talking, stop moving, rest, shut up....

KNOW....see, be aware, realize, acknowledge, understand...

So be STILL... stop trying to fix it yourself but instead REST in Him KNOWING... not doubting, questioning, worrying, fearing, wondering, hoping, fretting, wishing... but KNOWING He has got you, sweet friend.

KNOW He is your EVERYTHING!

KNOW He is your Provider!

KNOW He is your Healer!

KNOW He is your Protector!

KNOW He is your help on the time of trouble!

KNOW He is your Waymaker!

KNOW He is your Savior!

KNOW He is your Strength!

KNOW He only wants what's BEST for you!

KNOW He loves you!

KNOW He will never leave you nor forsake you!

KNOW He is your peace!

On this gut wrenching and quite horrible evening, somehow I was able to see the beauty. I was able to see that He had me, and I only needed to be still and know.

Be still and know that I am God; I will be exalted among the nations, I will be exalted in the earth!

—Psalms 46:10 NIV

Summary

How often do we miss the opportunity to invite Jesus into our situation from the very beginning? How different would things look? We find ourselves mentally, emotionally, and even physically exhausted and stressed because we are trying to fix the problem alone. We rely on our own knowledge, our own flesh and selfish ways to bring understanding and peace, when all the while He is our answer. Why do we wait until we can't take it any longer—THEN our heart begins to cry out for help? What if we called upon the Lord in the waking hours of our situation instead? I've come to find that there is such stillness and immediate comfort to be found when He is in it from the very beginning. Why wait a single minute to usher the King of Kings and the Lord of Lords into your life-shattering news? My heart hurts for those who never realize that sweet peace can take over, when you can't stand, when you can't even breathe.

Let the love of Jesus surround you, and in that stillness, you will feel His loving arms holding you tight.

He is there, invite Him in.

I Shall Not Fear

I thought faith would say, I'll take away the pain and discomfort, but what it ended up saying was, I'll sit with you in it.

—Brene Brown

Fear makes the gap between where I am and trusting God seem impossible. Paralyzing fear.

Been there? I have. I've been SO fearful that I remember mentally and emotionally crawling into a hole.

I know fear.

I know fear as a child.

I know fear as an adult.

I know fear as a parent.

I know paralyzing fear. I'm so thankful that is only a faded memory for me. I've learned to trust. But it's definitely not always been that way.

God, I know you're with me but why can't I see or feel that you are? Dealing with a child who has battled a long-term illness since he was 12 years old hasn't always been easy as it is now that he's an adult. I remember the long and lonely nights when he wanted to be a typical child and have sleepovers with friends, cousins or even his grandparents. It was one of the hardest things as a mom I ever went through. Letting him go, encouraging this fun loving, right and tough little boy to go have a good time and make memories. As he was packing his bag, I could feel the fear begin to swell up into a very present hard knot in my throat making it hard to even swallow at times. I would fight back the tears as I would get in my car and drive away after dropping him off. I am his mama; I was supposed to be there by his side in case he needed me.

On those long, lonely nights, I would awaken and find myself in a panicked state. Early in the diagnosis I'd felt the fear so strongly I would reach for the phone and call the place where he was staying just to check on him and make sure everything was okay. I couldn't sleep until I knew. This of course would be in the wee hours of the morning.

(I'm sure they all appreciated that wake up call.)

Finally, I got to the place where I would call on the Lord instead. I found myself praying this prayer over and over, "Lord, I can't be with him but I know you are. Protect him, Jesus, and keep him from falling into a diabetic coma." I knew he heard me. I knew he had dispatched angels and placed them around my child to keep him from harm.

My trust in Him was growing stronger.

My confidence was stretching into a strong belief.

My faith was growing.

I thanked him.

When gratitude began to flow from my heart, praise would spill out of my mouth, then it would happen. An undeniable peace ALWAYS followed, and I would drift back off to sleep.

Way too quickly this little boy grew into a handsome, strong college student. The past three years he has been five hours away from home attending a small Christian college to pursue his calling in the ministry. Have there been moments I worried, as all mamas do when their young adult leaves home and attends college? Oh yeah! But then add in the fact that his diabetes is still very present and is a constant and daily battle to control the roller coaster ride of highs and lows. But I must say that those lessons learned along the way to trust Him sure have come in handy all these miles away.

The only way I have learned to move beyond this helpless, hopeless, and miserable state I've found my pitiful self in from time to time through the years, is through prayer, praise and gratitude.

When I stopped and looked around, I saw Him.

I saw that he really was there.

He was in a smile from a stranger, a kind word, or a song on the radio. I could see him. I often go on walks in the summer, and I intentionally look at my surroundings so I can see Jesus. I see him in the beautiful sunsets, the weeds in the ditch, the cattle in the pasture and the clouds in the sky. Stopping to thank him for a beautiful day, the chirping birds or the warm sun I feel on my cheeks.

Gratitude and thankfulness ALWAYS move me beyond my circumstances into a place of feeling, seeing, realizing he has never left me nor forsaken me. He IS with me, always.

Remembering what God has done in the past for you is the secret to finding strength for today's and tomorrow's battles. What a beautiful gift. God does not want us to stay paralyzed in fear. He has equipped us with comfort and reassurance. Over and over throughout the Bible, he tells us NOT to fear.

Maybe you are walking through a storm right now or perhaps you see a storm on the horizon, take comfort in the fact that He will never leave you. You may not always feel him, you may not always see him, you may not always find the words to be thankful. As the old hymn says... Great is thy faithfulness, Lord unto me.

> **Have I not commanded you? Be strong and courageous. Do not be afraid; do not be discouraged, for the Lord your God will be with you wherever you go.**
>
> —Joshua 1:9 NIV

Summary

You just read..."I am with you." I wish I could tell you are always going to be comforted. But sometimes fear is so present, the words that could or should penetrate your heart and soul in trusting and comforting ways just don't. Sometimes they even make you angry. It's hard to fathom that God is with you when your pain is so great, when your world is falling apart, when your struggle is so real, when the healing hasn't come. But just know that He is a good father who will meet you where you are and who will never leave you.

Ingrid's Story

She never seemed shattered; to me, she was a breathtaking mosaic of the battles she's won.

—Matt Baker

I took a seat on the couch. Smoothed the imaginary wrinkles in my skirt. Shallow breaths. Something wasn't right.

I had been dropped off at a recently married friend's house. We had planned for a day of shopping, lunch, and a mini road trip.

She stepped into her bedroom to finish getting ready. That's when I heard it. When I felt it. When I wanted to run from it.

Control. The dark kind.

I nervously waited. Not knowing what to do as the voices got louder. My heart was pounding. Do I run to the kitchen and call someone? Who do I call?

Then I heard her cry out. Commotion. Things falling from a dresser. A loud thud.

Silence.

He walked out and stopped halfway across the room to glare and me and say, "Some people just need to be taught a lesson." His words were empty. A cowardly attempt at justification. I immediately despised him. Then he was gone.

That was the first time I knew my sweet friend Ingrid was fighting a battle so foreign to me.

Over the years there would be babies, moves, times of losing touch and then moments of reconnecting. It was always there in her eyes. The hurt. The hopelessness. The defeat.

As many women who have been in an abusive relationship have experienced, the breaking point was when she saw what this was doing to her kids at tender ages. The proverbial last straw was when, in front of her kids, he threw her out. A wounded heap of blood, bruises, missing hair, and tears.

Numb. Her only clear thought was getting the kids out of there.

She mustered up enough strength to go to the police. Pictures. Warrants. Waiting. He would take her kids and run. Determination won over worry. Prayer swept fear aside. And then, after three days her kids were back in her arms.

The beginning of the end. The end of being controlled. The end of walking on eggshells. The end of living in fear.

I had seen a new side of her for years on social media. He was out of the picture. Her kids were safe. Her silent strength now roared.

Several years back we were able to see each other in person. She stood with confidence and calm. Her smile reached her eyes. She told how her precious kids were thriving. Building churches, ministries, and strong families. Trauma may have tried to take them out, but it stood no chance against the God that formed them.

Now they soar. Now she lives a vibrant life. Helping others is her driving force. Resilience rose up within her. She was always brave. Now she is unstoppable.

> ***You intended to harm me, but God intended it all for good. He brought me to this position so I could save the lives of many people.***
>
> —Genesis 50:20 NLT

Summary

My friend, if you are reading these words today and any of this is hitting home with you, reach out. Talk to someone. Stand tall and fight for your safety and that of your children.

You are not alone. You are not damaged. You are not worthless.

You are loved. You are beautiful. You have purpose.

I wish I knew why these things happen in life. I don't. No magic words. Just the incredibly courageous story from a friend whose broken, pain filled, and tumultuous world became one of joy, love, redemption and peace. Never lose hope.

Lessons

IN MEMORY OF MY MOTHER-IN-LAW LIBBY
BURTRON

**Sometimes things that hurt you the most,
teach you the greatest lessons in life.**

—Unknown

She started teaching at a young age.

A Teachers' Aid for 30 years.

A Sunday School teacher for over 40 years.

A Mother, teaching her own.

A Grandmother, leaving a legacy and a blueprint for generations to come.

I sat by the bedside of my mother-in-law just a few short years ago. After a ten-year battle of Parkinson's Disease and dementia, her battle was coming to an end.

The facility we so hated having her in had called the family to be by her bedside. We had been here before but this time it felt different. This time in my heart I knew it would be the last call. We were told we just had a few hours to be with her so if there was anything you wanted to tell her one more time, this was the opportunity. So, like most families do, we made the dreaded phone calls to let everyone know. One by one her children, their spouses, her grandchildren, and her sister filtered through. We waited for the last breath to be taken. For the heavenly host of angels to carry her through the gates of Heaven. The clock continued to tick. Soon evening was drawing near and little by little the family made their way back home. What was a few hours left, so we thought, ended up turning into a few more days. Then when God decided it was her time, he called her home.

I'll never forget those few days that we spent by her side.

All the lessons she taught us during that most difficult time will be remembered forever.

The lesson that God is in control.

The lesson that His ways are not our ways.

The lesson to trust the Lord in all things.

The lesson that in hardship there is beauty and in pain there is a blessing.

The lesson called trust.

The lesson called patience.

The lesson to cling to Jesus for your comfort.

The lesson of such sweet and perfect peace.

The lesson to finding joy through the tears.

The lesson in knowing we would see her again.

The lesson in the waiting taught me firsthand where my strength comes from. The lesson in waiting taught me to let go of everything and just sit... and wait.

There was nothing I could do, it was all in HIS timing, I was not in control. Waiting in the sorrow, in the storm, in the trial is not where you want the be.

We as humans typically want to rush and get past it. We like the other side of the storm. But I found the beauty of the lessons to be learned, if we allow it, during the storm. These lessons are the ones that will help you throughout the rest of your life. The lessons that you will pass down to your children and grandchildren. The lessons that even in death are there to be learned.

A teacher until the very end.

A teacher I'm still learning from today, tomorrow and for all the days of my life.

*I have fought the good fight, I have
finished the race, I have kept the faith.*

—2 Timothy 4:7 NIV

Summary

Life is full of surprises and curve balls. Life is full of challenges and heartache, but in those moments there are so many lessons to be learned. Look for the lessons, glean from them, apply them. Choose to accept the lessons and you'll find that those lessons also come with abundant joy, peace, and happiness.

A Dream

When you cease to dream, you cease to live.

—Unknown

Shy.

Quiet.

Introvert.

Happy.

Sometimes when I see a picture of this little girl, I wonder what she was destined to be.

What was her purpose?

Where would she go in life?

How was God going to shape and mold her?

Who would she marry?

What would she do?

Would she have children?

Where would she live?

Of course, no one could have known for sure how life would go, but rest assured this little girl was told often how much she was loved. That she could be or do anything she wanted to. That the Lord loves her. She was given every opportunity to blossom into a confident grown woman. Yet during adolescence and those rough teen years she didn't believe it. She didn't think she was smart enough, pretty enough, strong enough or good enough. Self-doubt crept in and brought with it fear. Fear of failure, fear of saying or doing the wrong thing. Fear of what others thought. Fearful of acceptance.

Tall, lanky, crooked teeth and teen awkwardness disappeared as adulthood approached. This little girl matured and grew into the confident woman you see today when you look at me. I grew in my faith and that brought the truth about who I was. It brought a maturity and an understanding of who God made me to be and it didn't matter anymore what others thought. When I found out who I was, it erased the doubt, the fear, and the poor self-image. I believed the truth. The truth that I WAS enough!

How many of us are bold enough to say as David did in Psalms 139, "I am amazing. I am a masterpiece." Those thoughts never enter most people's minds. They are too busy putting themselves down, focusing on flaws, comparing themselves to others whom they think are better. I know how this works... because that WAS me.

Think on this: your Painter, your Creator, says, "You're amazing. You're wonderful. You're a masterpiece." You just have to believe it. You have to accept that he doesn't make junk. He doesn't create flaws. Think about what you'd say to that little girl, with a shy smile and big brown eyes. Would you tell her she not good enough, she's not smart enough, or she's ugly. Would you tell YOUR "little" self these things? NO!!!! You wouldn't dare tell a child that would you? Then listen to me. STOP telling yourself that now as the "big" girl. Mamas, you are that same person. God made YOU to be who YOU are!!! It's time to get into agreement with God.

Say it: I am a masterpiece. I am a child of the Most High God! I am beautifully and wonderfully made. Now go and BELIEVE it! Go and LIVE it!

A few years ago, I sat in the audience of about 12,000 people at a convention in Las Vegas. I was admiring and watching a selected few hundred successful men and women walk across the big stage and receive acknowledgement for their hard work and achievements. I said to myself and those around me, "I WILL be up there next year." Well, it didn't happen. That wasn't God's plan. But the dream was birthed, nonetheless.

A dream that one day I'd be on this stage being recognized for my achievements.

A dream that would represent thousands of lives changed for the better.

A dream that would be life changing for my family.

A dream that was transforming me into what He wanted me to be.

A dream that launched purpose.

A dream that had me driving a Lexus, earning a six-figure income and annual earned trips and prizes along with a lot of responsibilities.

A dream that would allow me to contribute to our family's needs, goals, and yes... even "wants".

A dream that would allow us to give and contribute to the needs of those less fortunate.

A dream that would allow time freedom.

A dream that would allow us to travel and live out our bucket list.

A dream that would provide residual income and a legacy for generations to come.

A dream that would allow me to bless the Kingdom.

A dream that God would use me in ways I would have never thought possible or could have imagined.

This dream became reality.

Four years after the dream was birthed deep in my heart, I walked on that same stage. I walked out there with a pounding heart, a smile as big as Texas, shaking knees and sweaty palms that made me almost dropped the microphone I was handed.

I was given a huge opportunity to share with the crowd of 15,000 how I had overcome and persevered with the Lord Almighty by my side. I had hit the top tier of my company. At this time, I was used in ways only HE could set up. I proclaimed the goodness of God. It was not about me and what I had done. It was ALL about Him and what He had done through me.

When you know it's the path He has set you on, NEVER lose sight of that. Put the blinders on and just do the work. He will bless it. He will use you, and He will make your dreams come true. This day, a dream came true. A God dream came true.

I woke up this morning and grabbed my cup of hot green tea like any other normal morning. I sat down and took a sip. I then saw the two powerful yet simple words printed on the side of one of my favorite mugs. "Dream Big." I had read these words many times in the past. This day they hit me a little different.

Self-doubts and all, dreams do come true.

> ***You are altogether beautiful my
> darling; there is no flaw in you.***
>
> —Song of Solomon 4:7 NIV

Summary

Dreams DO come true, and when coupled with hard work and prayers, the blessings and the favor of God bring your dreams to life. When you surrender your flaws, self-doubt, will, and ways to Him, you will soon find yourself not just living the dream but realizing that God's plan was far greater than the dream you had to begin with. Dare to dream friends, and dream BIG.

Bittersweet Blessings

IN MEMORY OF MY MOM SANDY ENGQUIST

Some days punch us in the gut so hard it seems we can feel the whole universe gasp with despair.

—Curtis Tyrone Jones

There it was again.

A thought. An ache to see family. A bizarre idea.

A recent historic storm packing 45 minutes of hurricane force winds had changed the geography of our city, displaced friends, and temporarily halted the return to any type of school.

So what is one to do with five kids already stir crazy from five months of quarantine/pandemic life?

Did someone say road trip??!!

Yep. Bizarre idea.

Charlie wanted to stay back with Everett as we had made the same trip to Phoenix in May after my mom had a traumatic fall that left her with multiple broken bones, hospitalized alone, and eventually moved to home hospice. Her muscle mass had been almost depleted from muscular dystrophy, so there were no interventions available. She was healing at home and still felt she would one day walk again.

My family loves surprises so I thought what better way to lift the spirits of my parents than a visit!?

Day one of the trip was uneventful and we made it to somewhere in Oklahoma. After sleeping for about five hours, I was ready to hit the road so four pajama clad kids gathered their things and followed me to the truck. One Venti Dark Roast later and we were on our way!

Well, after our 756th stop of the day we made it to Holbrook, AZ. While waiting for Baja Blasts for the kids I was trying to calculate our arrival time and driving through the mountains time! Not a fan of the latter so wanted to make sure it was still daylight.

As we approached Pine (the cutest little mountain town) I noticed the sun beginning to set and then remembered the time change. Twenty minutes later, it was night driving.

So... I have one good eye. One. That makes for depth perception issues at times. I stayed in the right lane and drove five miles under the speed limit much to the chagrin of my children who called me boring.

All was fine until the weather alert blared from my phone and all five of us had instant PTSD from the Derecho! Within minutes while rounding a high curve the skies opened, traffic came to a halt, and we were huddled against the wall of a mountain while two lanes over it was the biggest cliff of the drive.

"Are we gonna blow over the edge??!!"

"Are we gonna die??!!"

"NO!!" (As I inch closer to hug the mountain.)

Then the hail began, and our heavy truck was shaking from the wind. Remembering a meme I had seen over the past few months I laughed and said, "Okay God! I'll go to Nineveh!!" Then the kids heard the story once again of Jonah and my modern-day current adaptation.

Someone once said that song writers and musicians don't often realize when a lyric sounds great but has a huge significant meaning... you better be ready at some point to live out what you are writing and singing!!

That brings me to this one. A favorite from almost 15 years ago.

I beg for you to move.

I beg for you to move.

I beg for you to break through.

Simple. Profound.

As I sat on that mountain thinking, "Well, what next?" I had zero expectation as to what would be next.

I had no idea our giggles and shouts of surprise would turn to wide eyes, soft voices, tears and a worried and broken heart.

I had no idea within a couple of hours my sweet mom would whisper, "It was a God thing you came when you did." She looked at me with those beautiful blue eyes that held unspoken words. Words she knew I didn't want to hear.

When she gathered enough strength she spoke of Jesus, of Heaven, of laying at His feet. She would look over towards me playing the piano and with a gleam in her eye and the slightest smile, she sang along in the softest voice.

She bragged about her kids.

She talked about music being her life.

She was saying farewell in the sweetest of ways.

The last several months of staleness in my heart was replaced with the emotional flooding of the here and now and the Hope of eternal life.

Trivial things faded.

He broke through.

Just not how I had thought.

Show grace. Love your enemy. Pray for those who hurt you. Be a servant. Talk to God. Beg for Him to move in your situation. Listen to His voice.

Follow the nudge. The one that tugs at your heart and won't go away. Yep, that one.

It may be your biggest breakthrough, or it may be your most bittersweet blessing.

As the rain and the snow come down from heaven, and do not return to it without watering the earth and making it bud and flourish, so that it yields seed for the sower and bread for the eater,
So is my word that goes out from my mouth: It will not return to me empty, but will accomplish what I desire and achieve the purpose for which I sent it.
You will go out in joy and be led forth in peace; the mountains and hills will burst into song before you, and all the trees of the field will clap their hands.
Instead of the thornbush will grow the juniper, and instead of briers the myrtle will grow. This will be for the Lord's renown, for an everlasting sign, that will endure forever.

—Isaiah 55:10-13 NIV

Summary

In a world that is filled with individuality there is still one thing that unites us. Storms. Natural like the one we encountered on the mountain and life's devastating tempests. They typically come as a surprise, or if we do get a warning, we have little time to prepare. We simply cannot control much that comes our way, yet we can control our reaction to them. It may be that all we can do is write a scripture on a sticky note and keep it where we have a daily reminder that we will be okay. We can hold a weary hand. We can shed some tears and share some memories. We can make a call or send a text. All it takes is looking into the eyes of fellow humans and we know one thing is for sure: We are not alone.

Sunshiny Day

IN MEMORY OF MY FATHER-IN-LAW CLAUDE
BURTRON

Never trust your fears, they don't know your strength.

—Athena Singh

It was a cold spring day. The kind of day that makes you feel like winter will never go away and spring is just a dream.

But the sun was shining. And not just shining, the sun was shining extremely bright on this particular frigid March day.

I had looked forward to this day for several weeks and it was finally here. It had been a year since Rhonda and I had been able to meet up. How excited we both were at the thought of finally being able to see each other, have some girl time, and to be able to focus on the task at hand. I had said my goodbyes to my sweet husband, finished my hot green tea, grabbed my suitcase, and got in the car to make the four-hour drive.

As I was backing out of our driveway, my cell phone began to ring and the caller ID showed "hubby." I quickly answered, thinking he forgot something and was letting me know he was headed back, or maybe he wanted to say he loved me one more time knowing I would be away for a few days. Instead on the other end I heard a nervous voice. It was hesitant. I knew immediately something was wrong. Then he said it. "Dad's been in an accident and he didn't make it".

I responded with, "Oh baby, I'm on my way." In disbelief I did what I only knew to do. I told him "It's gonna be okay..." and repeated, "I am on my way."

Then we hung up and I began to pray. Within a couple minutes I was at the scene of this tragic accident. I couldn't put the car in park and jump out quickly enough. I had to get to him and reassure him that we would get through this. I needed to hold him. I needed to look into his eyes and tell him we would get through this and that the Lord would be our strength.

Again, I noticed the bright sun.

For the next couple hours we stayed at the scene. I remember feeling helpless but tried my best to bring comfort to the horrific situation. It was so hard to try and grasp what had just happened.

Over and over we asked, "Why?" Over and over we asked, "How did this happen?"

Over and over we wiped our tears.

Boy, was it cold, but the sun was still shining so brightly.

We called the kids to tell them their Grandpa was gone. Oh, how tough that was.

To see and hear their sadness, their brokenness and their grief was so very heart breaking.

This wasn't the first time for our family to lose a loved one. As a matter of fact, just two days and two years earlier, my sweet mother-in-law had gone to be with the Lord.

Now my in-laws were together again and in each other's arms forever. Oh, what peace would flood our souls and broken spirits when we began to think of the reunion that just took place in Heaven on this cold spring day.

Over the course of the next few days, weeks, and months we found that grief would pay us a visit. It would come in waves and crash hard and furious. Sometimes in sweet subtle ways. The grief was ever so present. The sounds of pain could be heard in the moans and the wailing. The pain could be seen in the tears that would trickle down our cheeks as we would reminisce and tell stories of days gone by.

You see, I have known grief. But this time it was a little different.

This time grief came with a sidekick called FEAR which wasn't completely foreign to me.

I knew this ugly feeling; this felt a little too familiar.

I knew it was not good.

I knew it would torment me, try to hold me captive and send me in a downward spiral.

I knew if I left it unattended it could be destructive.

Fear of losing another loved one to a tragic car accident.

Fear I would get a life changing phone call again.

Fear that wanted to captivate my thoughts in the wee hours of the morning and accompany my thoughts as I went about my day.

Fear that would make my heart skip a beat, take my breath away, make my chest tight and steal my joy.

Fear that would keep my mind in overdrive, prohibiting me from peacefully falling asleep at night.

Fear that was causing me to think the worst in every situation.

Fear that was challenging my usual "positive" outlook on life.

You see I was allowing fear to overpower me to the point that it was becoming toxic. When fear becomes toxic, we can become paralyzed by all the what-ifs.

What if my spouse dies?

What if something happens to one of my kids?

What if something happens to my parents?

What if something happens to me, and my children are left without a mom?

But after a while, fear becomes a burden that just seems too heavy to bear any longer, so fear becomes paralyzing. Fear begins to take root in our lives and prohibits us from living joyfully, happy, fulfilled, victoriously and walking in our purpose. Fear becomes a distraction from our calling. Fear can be the lingering gnat that won't go away.

Let me remind you, I had already overcome fear in the past. God had done a work in my heart and mind in dealing with my son's diagnosis years prior. Who am I kidding, my childhood and adolescent years were full of fear. What I had learned through the years was that I have access to a trustworthy Father.

I knew I could place my worries and anxiety into the palm of God's hand and I would be just fine. My trust in God was strong, so I thought. So why was I struggling so much with fear, yet again?

Then slowly the sun began to shine bright within my spirit as I listened to the voice of God instead of the voices of the adversary.

For God hath not given us the spirit of fear; but of power, and of love, and of a sound mind. —2 Timothy 1:7 KJV

I remembered that it came down to choices I could make.

I could choose to trust God with my fears, or I could continue to listen to the voices of the enemy. After all the enemy knew exactly what he was doing. He knew that he could not bring me down with other vices, but that fear had always been a weakness of mine. Oh yes, Satan knew exactly what he was doing.

This made the choice for me very simple; I knew that I had to seek God until he took my fears away.

By choosing to trust God with my fears I found myself saying, "God, you know I struggle with this fear, but I choose to trust you anyway. I am going to invite you into my inner world and ask that you help me to feel peace." I also found myself inviting the Lord into rescuing me by reciting and sometimes even singing a line to a song that we would sing frequently at our church, "I have no reason to fear. The Lord is my light, the Lord is my light."

I began to seek Him by reading what He has to say through the Bible.

I would seek Him through prayer.

I would seek Him through the testimonies in my own life and others, where fear once stood, but had been replaced with peace.

I would seek Him by reminding myself of who He is and who I am in Him.

With each passing day and with each choice being made, I was being set free from the prison cell of fear. True freedom comes from fully relying on His promises and truly trusting God. When you are able to do this, fear will begin to lose its grip on you.

We are approaching the second anniversary of when the Lord called my father-in-law home on that cold sunshiny day. It took me a while, but I came to realize that grief doesn't have to have a partner.

Fear is dark and cannot exist where the sun shines bright.

That day will always be remembered as a day our hearts were broken. It will also be a day to remind us that life's darkest moments are no match for the brilliance of His love.

*Fear thou not; for I am with thee: be
not dismayed; for I am thy God: I will
strengthen thee; yea, I will help thee;
yea, I will uphold thee with the right
hand of my righteousness.*

—Isaiah 41:10 KJV

Summary

You will certainly go through some difficult times. But you do not have to be afraid of them because God has not given you a spirit of fear, but of power and of love and of a sound mind.

We can literally drive ourselves crazy with fear. Or we can break up with fear by making the choice to trust God with that fear, then seek Him until our fear subsides.

Just think about that with your fear. One day you can wake up and say, "I am not afraid. I sought the Lord, and He answered me. He delivered me from all of my fears."

Is today that day? May the sun shine upon you and give you peace.

The Wound We All Felt

If you owe someone an apology, tell them you are sorry today. If someone asks for your forgiveness, forgive them. Start being the person you always wanted to be today and don't waste your time worrying about tomorrow.

—Mary Kate McErlean
(father killed on 9/11 when she was 8
years old)

We had been in the air about ten minutes when the captain's voice filled the cabin. His tone was different than earlier.

He said two commercial airliners had hit the World Trade Center Buildings in New York. He said we needed to remain in our seats for the duration of the flight.

Silence.

I leaned my head against the window, staring into the most beautiful blue sky. Tears fell. My heart ached. Questions were swirling in my head.

I was in the first row and no one was beside me except for a man in a business suit across the aisle. I saw sadness in his eyes as he looked up for a moment from The Wall Street Journal.

The flight attendant was overly chatty, complaining that she would possibly miss her next flight.

The captain's voice again. He said the Pentagon had been hit by a plane.

Quiet mumbling. Crying.

This was a plane full of people from Washington. We all probably knew someone who worked at the Pentagon.

Minutes felt like hours.

Our captain's voice again informing us we were flying over Pennsylvania and would be without communication with ATC for the next ten minutes or so.

Only later would I understand the significance of that.

A smooth, uneventful landing. Federal agents escorting us to baggage claim. I turned on my phone to numerous messages and missed calls. I called my loved ones.

"I'm okay."

Chaos involving bags and vehicles turned to a hush as a small screen in baggage claim became a point of fixation for everyone.

We stared in disbelief.

Life would never be the same.

Weeping, hugging, offering rides to one another.

Shoulders straightened.

Jaws were set.

Determination could be seen.

Strength filled the room.

I saw some of the best of humanity that day even though it's possible I had walked by the worst of humanity earlier that day at airport security.

I spent the next couple of days with my parents who lived just a couple of hours away. Fear tried to weave its way into my heart but determination won. Evil would not win.

I drove to St. Louis to pick up my husband who was stranded on a business trip and we drove back to

Northern Virginia.

Within a few days I needed to get back on a plane to conduct a training in Chicago. As I nervously browsed the terminal gift shop, I decided to grab a card and some big bags of M&M's for the flight crew. This had to be a day full of emotions for them also.

Upon boarding I handed them the card and candy and found my seat. After a few minutes the captain began usual announcements then proceeded to read my card.

A few minutes later a flight attendant stopped by my row and with tears in her eyes explained why he had read it and why it meant so much to them.

Earlier that morning the entire crew had been at a memorial service in New York for their colleagues who lost their lives. This would be their first working flight since that dreadful day. We hugged and cried and proceeded to have an uneventful flight.

Each year when the anniversary of 9/11 rolls around, I think back on that day and the way we rallied around each other.

All differences were set aside.

It's true that won't forget. We can't.

To those who lost their lives.

To the families who are still broken and hurting today.

To friends and colleagues traumatized by thé events of that day.

We remember you.

We always will.

Come to me, all you who are weary and burdened, and I will give you rest.

—Matthew 11:28 NIV

Summary

9/11 will always be one of those days in which most people can tell you exactly where they were and what was happening in their life the moment they heard the news. It was a day of collective grief within our nation and our world. When we hurt so deeply and so suddenly, it truly does something within the heart. If we could take away one thing from that awful tragedy it would be to just love. Love your neighbor. Love your enemy. Love those who think differently than you. Love your family. Love is a powerful force and is probably the remedy of all remedies to heal life's greatest hurts. There will always be pain, tragedies, and devastation, but there will also always be a place of healing, restoration, and love for each and every person on this incredible journey called life.

A Little While

No winter lasts forever, no spring skips its turn.

—Hal Borland

I am coming to you today from my comfy spot on my patio, the Adirondack chair that faces the sunset. On any given summer evening this is where you'll find me. Just as my favorite season, Summer, is coming to an end; so are these long days. Living in the North gives me such great appreciation for sunny and hot days like today, I do my best to soak it in while I can.

Just like weather changes, new seasons of life aren't always enjoyable either. Sometimes the changes of life can create a feeling of insecurity, uneasiness and for many it comes with a companion, fear.

At the beginning of the New Year, 2021, I knew it was going to be a year full of change.

Our daughter was getting married in July and leaving the only home she'd ever known in her twenty-five short years of life. No more laughter or footsteps coming from her room. No more getting to see her beautiful face every single day. No more hearing the tunes of the few songs she plays so well on the piano. If I dwelled on the "no mores" I would be curled up somewhere with uncontrollable tears.

While this was such a beautiful and happy time in her life, it was bittersweet for mama. And I wondered: What would our new normal look like around here? How would we all handle the adjustment?

I knew our son was going to have a very invasive and major jaw surgery that would require us to be displaced in another state for two solid weeks. Less than one week from returning home we would be taking him back to college five hours away. Okay no big deal, right? Wrong. We/he was still managing his cruel and very slow recovery and road to healing.

Again, my mind wondered. How would he do through all of this? What would life look like with neither of my children home now? How would he settle into a new year of dorm life and classes under these circumstances?

I knew there were going to be some significant changes in my husband's career path and steppingstones that he would have to walk, as one chapter closes and another one opens.

What would this even look like for him or for us?

On top of our challenges, significant changes came to all three of my siblings' lives all within thirty days, obviously not affecting me directly, but causing me to have the thought of "change" on my mind.

I knew life would throw us curve balls we would have to dodge and uncharted waters we'd have to tread.

After all, that's life, right?

Seasons teach us that the one constant in life is... CHANGE.

I am someone who doesn't mind change, but man, this was a LOT all at once.

I found out that no matter how prepared I thought I was, or how much I thought I knew about the change that was about to take place, I still found myself holding on for dear life. Breathing heavily and on the brink of an emotional breakdown at times.

Holding on to the part and pieces that felt safe, felt normal and what felt comfortable instead of dwelling on the uncertainty and the fear attached to it.

Fear is a natural response to the unknowns that accompany transition, to all that we cannot control or predict, especially regarding the welfare of our family.

But to THRIVE in transition we must not freeze in fear of potential outcomes.

Acknowledging fear is the first step in moving forward courageously.

In this season of change for my little family and becoming semi-empty nesters, I surprisingly found such joy.

I found peace and overwhelming gratitude.

Oh, how a heart of gratitude and thankfulness can change your perspective.

Gratitude for what once was and what's to be.

Gratitude that I've been blessed to witness my babies grow up and fly from the nest.

I never want to be so wrapped up in resisting change and learning to embrace the new normal that I rob myself of the beautiful gift I've been given in the now. The today.

If you are in a season of change and feeling the weight of it, are grieved because of it, I have good news.

It will not be forever.

Things are going to change.

It may not seem like it, but that season will come to an end.

Maybe you're not in a "hard" or "life changing" season right now, but when you are, never forget it is only for a little while.

> **To *everything there is a season, a time for every purpose under heaven*.**
>
> —Ecclesiastes 3:1 KJV

Summary

Whatever season you find yourself in, this is your season for this time. God has a plan.

Learn to welcome change and enjoy it the best you can, in doing so you will be able to see the beauty in the season you are in.

It is there.

Choose to see the change as positive and keep the negative emotions in check. Feel them but move on.

Talk to others who've gone through the same changes and learn from their experience.

Above all, pray and pray a lot.

God will give you the peace your troubled heart needs.

I like the phrase "a little while." That tells me the season is going to end.

It is not forever. Every season ends. Winter ends. Spring ends.

Summer ends. Fall ends.

Every season has a beginning, and every season has an end.

His Last Mile

IN MEMORY OF MY GRANDPA WAYNE
GASTINEAU

If you love deeply, you're going to get hurt badly. But it's still worth it.

—C.S. Lewis

It was a day that began like all of the others, for my Grandpa. I imagine he turned back the covers, and slowly put his feet to the floor. Without thinking, he put one step in front of the other... down the short hall to the kitchen. He may have checked on a load of laundry he accidentally left in the dryer. Grandma would never go for that! He had better turn it back on to fluff the clothes again.

Taking a few more steps, he is in the kitchen where so many memories come to mind. He can almost hear the laughter of the grandkids at Christmas as they run through, on their way out the door for some football in the snow. He smiles as he looks at the table and remembers it set for the perfect breakfast.

For some reason, everything seems nostalgic today. Then he looks at the clock and realizes he had better hurry and get ready. He wants to pick Grandma up at the nursing home a few minutes early today.

You see, today is a bit special because he has been asked to speak at church. He makes sure his notes are in his Bible. A few minutes later, he is out the door, and starting the van. He stops by his favorite donut shop, and says hi to everyone there, and as he leaves, says a prayer under his breath for the man sitting alone at the counter, and for the weary cashier who is learning to be a single mom.

He arrives to pick up my grandma and she gives him a kiss on the cheek while patting his other cheek and somehow today... it reminds him of the first time she kissed him. She asked him to check the back of her hair, and he fumbles around with the pins and the flower and puts everything in its place. There, pretty as a picture!

He places his weary hands on the wheelchair, and with one foot in front of the other... he pushes his wife of almost sixty years down the long hall. He says Good Morning to a few people... asks them how they are doing. He smiles at the nurse behind the desk and says, "I am going to take Betty out for lunch today, so we'll be back later this afternoon." With a quick wave, he rolls my grandma out the door and onto the waiting lift to put her in the van.

On the way to church, they talk a little bit, but he is already thinking about how he is going to say some of the things that God has put on his heart to talk about. Just a simple life testimony, which is what he has decided to do. But, he wants to make it count. It has to touch someone...that is his prayer.

They turn into the parking lot, he shuts off the engine and gets Grandma, and begins his walk up the ramp... one foot in front of the other, he prays as he walks... wondering who will be there today that needs to hear his testimony?

The door opens, and his friend of many years is there to welcome them in. He finds his way to their seat, gets settled in and then takes a seat, just to rest and think for a few minutes before church starts. He looks around and his mind wanders. He can recall like it was yesterday... laying the carpet in this beloved church. His eyes look up and he wishes he could maybe pull his banjo out today. So many good times were had, playing his banjo with the worship band.

The church starts to fill up, the service begins. He is soon lost in the words to one of his favorite songs. Today is a good day. He can feel it from somewhere deep inside. After a few more songs, it's time for him to speak. The Pastor calls his name.

He takes a deep breath, grabs his notes, and puts one foot in front of the other... and makes his way to the front. As he rests his hands on the pulpit, it's like he felt God's hands resting on his shoulders. He begins to speak, and oh, does he speak. Gentle, with love, with humor, he tells his story.

About halfway through, the Hands he felt on his shoulders, now are taking his own hands, and are leading him one foot in front of the other, to a place that he has dreamed of for so long. Wasn't he just singing "Oh, I Want to See Him?"

He wishes he could tell his family and friends goodbye, but then he smiles and remembers... his notes. They will tell everyone goodbye... they will finish his story.

And so... he takes the Hand of His Maker and puts one foot in front of the other... he is home.

> ***If it be possible, as much as lieth in you, live peaceably with all men.***
>
> —Romans 12:18 KJV

Summary

A week or so later, his pastor read the rest of my grandpa's notes at his homegoing service. It was one of my most cherished times in God's presence. One of my grandpa's favorite songs was The Last Mile, and I have often thought of his own last mile... and decided to share how I imagine his day went.

It makes me realize that every day, every decision, every word, and every step we take should be for the good of others.

We often let the cares, stresses or even busyness of life take over, and we forget just why we are here. It may be to fluff some clothes in a dryer, it may be cooking dinner, it may be saying hello to the clerk at the dry cleaners, it may be punching a clock, it may be dispensing medicine, it may be sending the kids off to school in time.

When your feet hit the floor tomorrow, and you put one foot in front of the other and are off to your busy day... may you touch the lives of all those whose paths you cross.

Red Dirt Road

Sometimes it's the smallest decisions that can change your life forever.

—Keri Russell

I am a preacher's daughter.

In fact, my father has been a Preacher and for that matter, a Pastor, my entire life.

Ministry is such a huge part of my entire family.

But it didn't always look this way.

My dad's family was far from God. In fact, my father and his siblings grew up without even having a Bible in their home. They were a rough bunch. I remember Dad telling the stories as a child of how he often witnessed fighting, cussing, drinking, parties and dances. He would tell of being spanked so hard that blood would pool into his shoes. He was yelled at, called obscene names by his father, and recalls having conversations with his twin brother that went like this, "I don't want to live like this, there has to be a better way."

Dad along with is twin, older brother and younger sister moved countless times across southern Georgia. They changed locations, schools, and jobs in search of better living conditions and perhaps better pay. Could it be that they were not satisfied and were in search of happiness too?

Dad's parents worked long and hard days in the cotton fields and later in life in the cotton mills. Hard workers and hard living. My Grandpa Johnny ran moonshine out of their home. In fact, the legendary Sheriff L. L. Wyatt visited their home and told Johnny that if he didn't stop running moonshine, he was going to arrest him. Some of the family actually did spend time in the county jail and even years in prison. Stabbings, cheating, shootings, and theft were no stranger to the Wilson family.

There just so happened to be a few family members who had given their life to Christ.

One day Aunt Dorothy and Uncle Bill drove for an hour down many country dirt roads to see my grandparents. They told them about Jesus and invited them to church. It was a one-hour drive each way and their dad, Johnny, committed to driving the family to church in Athens the very next Sunday and every single Sunday thereafter. Dad told me, just a few years ago, that when his family stepped inside of this little country church, they felt loved. He said Daddy began to talk a little differently, the family began to clean up the way they were living and began to seek the ways of the Lord.

They decided to follow Jesus.

One day and one commitment changed the trajectory of my family.

Dad's family had very little, but they now had Jesus, and Jesus changed everything.

Because Aunt Dorothy and Uncle Bill shared the gospel of Jesus Christ with my grandparents, my dad made the decision to follow Christ. This was over 65 years ago. He was not only saved but he was called to the ministry at the young age of 14 and has been in ministry ever since. Because of this one decision to follow Christ, his ministry has produced many Pastors, Missionaries, Sunday School Teachers, Worship Leaders, Christian Authors, and hundreds to thousands who've become believers and Christ followers.

I love my father's story. It's one of forgiveness, grace, mercy, healing, and love. It's one that touches my heart to the core and has me so very grateful. Grateful for the decision that was made on that one day. Grateful for those who are obedient to their calling to share the gospel. Grateful to a God who saves. I often think, where would I be if the gospel wasn't shared on that day? Where would I be if my Grandparents hadn't made the decision to take their family to church? Where would I be if my father decided it wasn't for him? Where would I be if it wasn't for God reaching down to save a young boy who desired a way out?

Daddy found an altar, he found love, he found a better way.

> *You intended to harm me, but God intended it for good to accomplish what is now being done, the saving of many lives.*
>
> —Genesis 50:20 NIV

Summary

I share my dad's story to convey the importance of ONE decision. One decision can change everything not only for you, but for generations to come. Choices and decisions you and I make daily really matter. The choices you make today influence your tomorrow. Many times, we don't stop and think about how our decisions can affect our children and our children's children.

You can be the difference maker.

You can be the generation changer bringing happiness, hope, healing, and love to those who are so desperately in need.

After all... **Jesus** changes everything!

Love Stays

IN MEMORY OF MIKE AND BRAD

**The reality is, you will grieve forever. You
will never 'get over' the loss of a loved one;
you will learn to live with it. You will heal
and you will rebuild yourself around the loss
you have suffered. You will be whole, but you
will never be the same again. Nor should
you be the same, nor should you want to.**

—Elizabeth Kubler-Ross

She grabs hold of the railing as she makes her way up the few steps, knowing that once she walks through the big double doors, a heaviness will wash over her once again.

She looks around the beautiful church, sees the sun glistening through the stained-glass windows, and she takes a seat on the old wooden pew.

This little church building carries so many memories, some heartwarming and dear and others some of most the painful times in her life.

She remembers her first unexpected goodbye. It was Christmas. Her dad had gone out to get a tree and never came back. No explanation, no warning. Just a goodbye that was never said. As a little girl, she wondered if it was somehow her fault. Growing up she was full of questions as to why, but she stayed a good sister, she stayed a loving daughter. She stayed.

Several years later, as a nervous teenager, she walks through those doors again. This time was met with disapproving glances and was verbally attacked and shamed by a father figure who disapproved of the precious baby she was now carrying. He emotionally walked away from her. She stayed a dedicated mommy to be.

Fast forward about fifteen years later, and once again, words were said, decisions were made, and she was left to raise three boys on her own. She stayed a stable force. She stayed working as a single mom. She stayed committed to Jesus. She stayed in prayer over her boys. She stayed.

Over the next twenty years or so, she loved her family and her friends without reservation and without conditions. She made the choice to always stay. That's what love does.

She had learned over the years that her Heavenly Father was truly one who would be with her always. He would stay and never walk away from her.

She stayed close to her phone. She stayed in touch. She stayed in prayer. She stayed in a position of support. She stayed their biggest cheerleader. She stayed close by her mom and sister. She stayed a friend even though miles separated them. She stayed a faithful servant to others. She stayed positive. Her heart breaking, she stayed a shoulder of strength through the tragic loss of her oldest boy. His untimely and sudden death rocked her world, but she stayed a mom full of love for her other two boys.

She reaches down to feel the worn wooden pew, closes her eyes, and the tears spill out. She is tired. Tired of pain. The unthinkable happened today. She is saying goodbye to her middle son. How can this be?

Grief is attempting to consume her, yet she glances over and sees another mom who recently lost her son just a few days prior. So she wipes her tears, stands up, and goes over to give her friend a hug.

She stayed full of compassion. She stayed empathetic.

She stayed true to who she was.

She stayed a friend who comforts.

She stayed a voice of concern.

She stayed remarkably hopeful.

Years of trauma tried its best to win but was no match against the power of The One who defines Love. The Author of her story since day one. The One who promised in His Word to never leave us. He stayed.

> *Be strong and courageous. Do not be*
> *afraid or terrified because of them,*
> *for the LORD your God goes with you;*
> *he will never leave you nor forsake*
> *you.*

—Deuteronomy 31:6 NIV

Summary

There are people you pass by every single day who are experiencing some of the worst heartaches of their life. You may be one of those to whom life has handed blow after blow. It may feel like you are at your weakest. It's in those moments we are made strong. Not by hardening our hearts or building walls but by leaning into our Heavenly Father. His strength can almost be tangibly felt in some of our weakest moments. It's just the reminder we need to know we are not walking this alone.

We love because He loves.

We forgive because He forgives.

We stay because He stays.

Hidden Wounds

There's nothing more calming in difficult moments than knowing there's someone fighting with you.

—*Mother Teresa*

It was a beautiful fall day, and we had our binders and coffee in hand as we made our way into our class. Each week we learned all kinds of things about the world of foster care and adoption. A world so foreign to us yet we knew we were exactly where we were meant to be.

I had felt fear and anxiety at times in my life, but never what I was about to hear...

Imagine being terrified of certain sounds, smells, environments and even textures, and having no recollection of the reason behind the fear.

Your leg shakes, you fidget, you can't stay seated, you shut people out, your heart races.

So you look frantically for something to neutralize the panic that is rising within. You shout angry short commands at someone who you know loves you unconditionally. You need their comfort, but your brain is literally not wired to properly seek safety, comfort, and love.

Instead, you push away as more confusion swirls in your mind. You feel your muscles tighten.

You have no idea what to do.

You have no idea why you feel this way.

You have no sense of reasoning, danger, or consequences.

So, you do what your 4-month-old self did in these moments.

You scream.

Your eyes widen.

You kick.

You cry.

You stiffen.

You rage.

Then eventually you rest. Your adrenaline has reached its peak. You are drained, mentally and physically.

You let the one who loves you unconditionally sit beside you. You grab an arm with both hands as your head rests on their shoulder.

And you still have no idea why.

This is what can happen to kids from hard places.

This is what can happen to trauma survivors.

The brain is magnificent. It stores everything we have ever experienced. Yet it knows that most couldn't handle full recollection of every detail of our lives.

Our memories may be suppressed, but our bodies aren't so forgetful.

Sometimes it's good to write down your entire history. From the time in your mother's womb until now. It is eye opening to make the connection between certain environments and feelings of anxiety.

Our world is seemingly in a mental health crisis. There are so many people hurting, suffering, and trying their very best just to get through the day.

They don't want to talk about it or perhaps wouldn't even know where to start.

There are kids filling up our schools who are hiding their pain under long sleeves, a contrived smile or in pages of a journal that no one will ever see.

It may seem hopeless, but we can start with a listening ear.

Saying hello.

Giving a real smile.

Inviting someone to hang out or have coffee.

Noticing that kid who nervously fidgets.

Showing grace when someone withdraws momentarily.

There is a passage from the Bible that is often read at weddings, but I think it applies so very much to the emotional well-being of all of us and those we love.

Love is patient and kind; love does not envy or boast; it is not arrogant or rude. It does not insist on its own way; it is not irritable or resentful; it does not rejoice at wrongdoing but rejoices with the truth. Love bears all things, believes all things, hopes all things, endures all things. Love never ends.

—1 Corinthians 13:4-7 ESV

Summary

This world we are living in can be a cruel one. School, work, the store, and even our own homes, are filled with people carrying the weight of anxiety, past trauma, emotional wounds, low self-esteem, and depression. It is so easy to flippantly pass judgement or compare your story to the perceived full story of another. That's the thing though: You can never truly know the inner workings of one's heart and mind. How they process the cards dealt them may look very different than your coping mechanisms. All we can do at times is to be there. Be present and offer prayers, words of encouragement or tangible assistance. At times you may need to be their voice and advocate fiercely. If you are a caregiver, friend, or family to someone with wounds of the heart, take care of yourself also. You and the one you love are amazing, brave, and stronger than you know.

Perfect Love

What is breaking you is also building you.

—Anonymous

I can remember the first time I felt it. The strong grip of fear. It had grabbed hold of my heart at the tender age of 4.

I had been dreaming and woke with such panic that I made a beeline for my parents' room and literally dove on their bed while screaming their names.

Over the years it would rise up on occasion. Usually at night or, as I got older, if I was alone. I recall so many nights tiptoeing into my parents' room as a teenager with a pillow and blanket and I would find a spot on the carpet near the bed to try and get some rest before morning.

I don't know the origin of such intense fear but I sure became familiar with the feeling.

My Dad would quote a scripture to me over and over.

Perfect love casteth out all fear. — 1 John 4:18

I am so grateful that my parents were patient with me, were not dismissive, and made sure I knew that I was unconditionally loved.

Fast forward 15 years. Everett and I had been married six years, and we made a move to Iowa. There were so many ingredients that led to a perfect storm in my emotional life at that time.

Fear returned with a vengeance. I had severe panic attacks that would hit within 5-10 minutes upon waking and last almost the entire day. I was often sent home from work because hives would cover my chest, neck, face, and hands. At times I couldn't function mentally.

There was one night that sleep eluded me, so I called home around 2:00 in the morning. My mom and dad listened, prayed with me and then he said, "Remember, Perfect love casteth out all fear."

Sometime over the next year a huge shift took place within me. I knew I was oh so flawed. I knew I could never be good enough or do enough to earn God's love.

That's the thing. It wasn't that I needed to figure out how to love God better. The only one capable of loving perfectly was God himself.

Once I caught a glimpse of the depth of His love for me, I was overwhelmed.

Love held Him to a cross.

Love found my eyes in the crowd below.

Love spoke my name when I thought He had left me. Love calmed my fears.

Love promised He would never leave me.

If you are feeling paralyzed by fear, anxiety, worry or the cares of life, I want you to know there is hope.

Find someone to talk to.

Read scripture.

Journal your thoughts.

Surround yourself with those you love.

You will one day find yourself on the other side of it although it may not look like it right now.

You may feel it's a never-ending battle.

You may feel you are broken beyond repair.

Choose to acknowledge the feelings but choose to believe the facts.

You are loved.

Wholly.

Unconditionally.

Beautifully.

That sounds pretty *perfect* to me.

> **The Lord your God is in your midst, a warrior bringing victory. He will create calm with His love; He will rejoice over you with singing.**
>
> —Zephaniah 3:17 CEB

Summary

Fears can come in all shapes and sizes. About 12% of adults in the US have specific phobias, approximately 35% have simply feared for their own safety within a mile from their home. Regardless of the degree and frequency, fear is something that makes us uncomfortable. Those who have never dealt with it on a regular basis struggle with understanding its grip. There are practical things to do as mentioned above. Taking walks, talking to someone, listening to calm music, creating a peaceful and safe space for yourself. You can also dig into God's word as it is full of stories and scriptures to help navigate foreboding waters. He is with you and will never leave you, despite what your feelings may be telling you. Trust His promise while tending to your anxious heart. Courage is within you and peace is just around the next bend.

At Home

IN MEMORY OF MY MOTHER-IN-LAW JUNE MCCOY

Hospitality is love in action. It is the flesh and muscle on bones of love. The heart of hospitality and the heart of God are the same.

—Henri Nouwen

Sometime in the spring of 1990, I nervously walked up a few steps and through the door into your kitchen. It was my first time to meet you and I will never forget how welcomed you made me feel.

I felt loved.

I felt at home.

The years brought many moves, distance, and changes. Several years later, life brought us back to living in the same town. My girls adored you from the moment we unpacked the moving truck. You were such a sweet Grandma to them.

Your other grandkids were grown and in different seasons of life, yet you welcomed three rambunctious toddler girls into your heart and life. You even bought them fun special cups they used when we would stop by. They loved your big bowl of popcorn, snuggling on the couch to watch a movie or pulling out the box of toys from years gone by.

They felt loved.

They felt at home.

We watched you host your famous "open house" each Christmas. You baked for days and pulled out all of your Christmas finest. Streams of people would walk through your door year after year. You always greeted them with a smile and made sure they knew you were so glad they stopped by.

They all felt loved.

They all felt at home.

When we heard your time with us would be cut short, it hurt to our very core. We had taken in two new kids just a few months earlier and you loved and cared for them so much. You made an impact on them in that short time. So much so that Lily took on your name to be her middle name on adoption day.

We miss you more than words can say. I know you wanted to help with editing this book and you were one of my biggest encouragers to even venture into the world of writing. I hope I have made you proud.

Although our hearts ache at your absence, we are filled with peace in knowing that you are resting in a place where you feel so welcomed.

You are loved.

You are at home.

> *He will wipe away every tear from their eyes.*
>
> —Revelation 21:4 NLT

Summary

There are times in life that we get so busy with what we are doing that we forget about others. We are taught to focus on our wants, goals, desires, and plans for a better life. That's all okay as long as it is balanced. Take time to carve out moments in which you do something for someone else just because. Open up your home, give a smile, take someone to breakfast, bake brownies for a bunch of teenagers, or make that phone call. Serving others has a lasting effect. You can make a difference in someone's life by simply making them feel loved and at home.

Tami's Final Thoughts...

As I am gathering my final thoughts today, my mind is wandering off to the areas of my life that were wounded, that were painful. Areas of my life that were so full of hurt, loss, change, and fear. These are the stories which I've shared with you on the pages of this book. Within each and every circumstance, I also wanted you to see that these trials of life were also so full of JESUS.

While my faith was shaken, at times to my core, I was standing on a firm foundation. Not only was I still standing, I was also marching. I marched on through those long and hard winter seasons of life because I had His hand to hold.

Psalm 16:8 NLT says, "I know the Lord is ALWAYS with me. I will not be shaken, for He is right beside me."

I can see that many of the wounds I've experienced through life and even in recent years, have turned into scars. Not just any scar, but beautiful scars. The scars are beautiful because I can see Jesus in them. I see the purpose in my pain.

Cancer could have taken me out.

Fear could have set up camp.

Discouragement could've settled in my spirit.

Instead, purpose was born.

The scar reminds me that Jesus used my brokenness to also bring me the breakthrough.

Did you know that God uses broken things? It takes broken soil to produce a crop, broken clouds to give rain, broken ground to get bread, broken bread to give strength. It is the broken alabaster box that gives forth perfume.

So, as I wrap this up, I want you to know that there is purpose in your pain.

Matthew 6:32 says that your Heavenly Father already knows. Jesus wants to reveal Himself as your Healer.

What does your scar look like?

Perhaps your wound isn't a beautiful scar just yet. Maybe your wound of grief, loss, loneliness, confusion, discouragement, change, sickness, heaviness, emptiness, brokenness, bitterness, rejection, abuse... the list could go on and on... has you feeling like there is no hope and no future.

As much as we all want to float through life without encountering hard times, the fact is most of us will face them.

And while the trials of our lives are not predictable in their intensity or length, they do point to the one who never changes and is always dependable—the same, yesterday today and forever.

Your strength CAN be restored and renewed... right smack in the middle of your hard season.

Peace and understanding CAN enter your mind... right smack in the middle of your storm.

God CAN direct your path and give you wisdom for your next step... right smack in the middle of your hard season.

One of the lessons I have learned in recent years is to slow down and soak in the moment, even in the open wound phase.

I've had this thought on my mind a lot lately. Maybe it's because my grown children have left the nest and are flourishing, just as I prayed they would when they were little. But how on earth did we get there so fast? This is a common topic with my husband, almost daily. Doesn't life seem to be moving at lightning speed these days? Why is that? How is that? What can be done about it? These are the questions that swirl around in my mind from time to time. I'm not sure we can stop the speed at which a day, a month, a year, or a decade comes and goes, but what we can do is control the time in which we choose to spend those minutes and hours that turn into days, months, years and even decades.

I fear that if we don't slow down and take the time to notice, soak in, and savor our moments and what we appreciate and value most, we will look back in time with many regrets. The "I wish, why didn't I, and if I could"... will dominate our thoughts and vocabulary.

I don't want to be that person. Instead, I want to look back over my life knowing that I captured the true essence of life itself.

I want to live in the moment. I want to be present and soak in every ounce of those I love.

Yep, even if I don't see the scar yet, let alone the beauty in the scar.

So much of life happens within the four walls of our home. We can set the mood in our home that nurtures our body, mind and soul so that we can actually "soak it in." It would be very difficult for us to be able to be entirely present if our mind isn't in the right place. If we are worried, filled with anxiety and fear, how can you set the tone of peace, joy, and happiness in the home if deep down you're not happy? If life is filled with chaos, turmoil and strife, there isn't room for happiness, peace, and contentment. Feeling good and being healthy is SO important too. If you don't feel well, it spills over into everything you do. If you're miserable, the atmosphere in your home will be toxic.

See how it all fits together? One thing can easily have such an enormous effect on another area of our life.

Remember the story I shared about taking my father back to Georgia a few years ago? We stood outside the church where he came to know the Lord and where he was saved. One of the most beautiful and unforgettable moments on this trip was when we took Dad to the Oconee River, where he had been baptized at the age of 14. I stood on the banks of the river and watched my dad wipe the tears from his eyes as he recalled that beautiful moment in his life. I had heard the story many times throughout my childhood, but standing there with him at that moment meant so much to him and possibly even more to me. Listening to my dad at the age of 78 relive this life-changing time was just so beautiful and will be treasured forever.

As we sat in the airport waiting on the return flight home to Indiana, I asked my dad, "What was the best part of the trip?" And he said, "Going to the river." I smiled, for that was my favorite part of the trip as well. That moment in time would not have been possible had I not made the trip.

I share a portion of this story with you again because I feel that someone might need to hear the words, "healing is in the doing."

Keep moving. Keep living. I intentionally chose to seize the moment with my aging father in the middle of one of the busiest and most challenging summers of my life. You see this was just months after losing my father-in-law in a horrific accident, in the middle of heavy grief and an extremely stressful time in in dealing with the in-laws' estate. Add in the fact that my son was finishing an internship and needing an answer to his next step and where he would put down roots with a job and eventually home to his bride. So many life-altering decisions and heaviness occupied my mind, yet I grabbed hold of the opportunity to take this trip, and in doing so it gave me the ability to keep marching on through life. This is when some turn to an addicting vice, lay crippled and afraid to move, look to "things" to fill the void or to be the answer. Sometimes just taking a step is all you need to do.

So, what are some things we can do to ensure we are living our best life, we are feeling our best, we are creating spaces and moments in our life and in our home to be able to "soak it in"?

Slowing down to savor solitude is very difficult. I have come to find the healing is often in the quiet.

Learn to say no without excuses so you can be more selective on how you spend your day. Guard your time.

Give yourself permission to live at a different pace from the pace of others around you.

Create a special place for self-care. Set up a comfortable chair and get a basket together for your books and journals for some quiet time.

Light candles to remind you to stay in the moment, journal your thoughts in pretty notebooks, meditate on gratitude and pray daily.

Get up a half hour earlier or stay up a half hour later to have some peace and quiet.

Be yourself and live authentically. Trying to impress is a great way to feel unbalanced and unhappy in life.

Get healthy. Stop the excuse that you don't have time to exercise. Be mindful of what you put into your body.

Create memory making moments.

Take the trip.

Take the scenic route.

Take a walk.

Sleep in.

Take a nice quiet bath in place of a quick shower.

Light a candle and sip on hot tea or your favorite cup of coffee.

Open a photo album and take a walk down memory lane.

Stop at a local park and go for a swing.

Go create the joyous memory that awaits you. By doing so, you may receive the healing you desperately need in that season.

Perhaps by slowing down and soaking in precious life moments, you'll be able to see the beauty and a fading scar.

Whether you prefer filling your home with the aroma of candles or baking, flowers or essential oils, there is nothing that replaces or that can set the tone in your home like Jesus can. Be sure to usher in His presence daily. Infusing your home and life with Jesus makes all the difference.

My hope and prayer for you today, as you close this book, is that you are encouraged, uplifted, and cling to the truth that Jesus makes Beautiful Scars.

When you don't see the beauty, I pray the Lord teaches you to depend on Him. I pray that you wait on Him, you learn from Him, and you give praise to Him for His faithfulness and for His constant promises.

When you don't understand life's difficulties, I pray you can still see and feel Jesus near.

Your healing will come, and you will see the beauty in the scar.

Rhonda's Final Thoughts...

As you have probably realized by now, our plans for this book encountered many detours. We always knew that God was still in this, and for some reason, unbeknownst to us, the book would be on hold time and time again.

So much so that we began to look at it as a story of its own. We started out to share some stories of how we made it through difficult moments and seasons of our lives, only to be hit with some of the darkest days smack dab in the middle of putting stories to paper.

We kept moving along, little by little, word by word, story by story, on His timeline.

Adversity is an interesting one. The very thing that breaks you can also be the thing that heals you.

This morning on the way to school, my daughter mentioned that one of her teachers has had a rough couple of years with family illness and unexpected deaths of friends.

Today I planned to sit down and pull together some closing thoughts to share with you. Hearing this was a reminder yet again that we are all in this thing called life together.

We have days and seasons of joy and celebration and yet pain will come to every one of us also. When we are at our lowest and weakest is often when we see another side of us that perhaps was previously hidden.

Strength.

Resilience

Determination.

Empathy.

Courage.

What a journey these last four years have been. Taking you through different moments in time when life hit really hard.

Thinking I was far enough removed from the initial pain that I could write about the healing process.

Then the unthinkable happened a few months into it. One of my life's biggest hurts to date. Losing my precious Momma.

My biggest encourager.

The one who told me for years that I needed to write a book. The one who always found good in me when there was none to be found.

I am still in the healing process. Maybe it is the wound that never really heals; yet lessons, purpose, and compassion have created a balm that soothes a broken heart.

Being given a lifelong illness or walking through devastation can shake us to the core. It's been said that it's not so much what happens but our reaction to it. So much easier said than done. My prayer is that whatever life has blown your way, you find a way to rise up in strength and determination, then go in the pursuit of what that voice inside is telling you to do.

You are not your diagnosis.

You are not your trauma.

You are an overcomer.

It isn't always easy to embrace reality and see it for the gift it is. Those many dark years of infertility and wondering what my life would eventually look like seemed to be all-consuming at times. As I look back now, I wouldn't have it any other way. The roadblocks led us to the exact path we are on today. Our home has evolved over the years and has been filled with all the emotions. People often say that our kids are blessed to have us, and I always reply that it is I who am blessed. I can't imagine a different path. To some it may look like a household of craziness, but it sure looks amazing to our Creator. All of it. The beauty, the mess, the joys, the mistakes, the hurts and, yes, even the healing.

My prayer is that you have found some inspiration for whatever season you find yourself in. Are you currently in the fight of your life? Hold on my friend. Let the healing begin, one tiny step at a time.

I don't have all the answers. I certainly don't have a magic formula for grief. We are all still a work in progress. Some days may be rough, others full of joy and excitement, some may be filled with heartbreak and tears, but one thing I have learned from wounds of the past... there is purpose in it all.

What lies down the road? Oh, how we wish we knew. Through the eyes of the One who created us and is the giver of all hopes and dreams, we can be assured... it will be oh so beautiful.

> *Now we see things imperfectly, like puzzling reflections in a mirror, but then we will see everything with perfect clarity. All that I know now is partial and incomplete, but then I will know everything completely, just as God now knows me completely*.

—I Cor 13:12 NLT

About the Authors

Rhonda is wife to Everett and mom to five beautiful children through foster care and adoption. She has been involved in worship ministry for most of her life, worked in the medical field for 25 years prior to becoming a Mom, and has always had a passion for expressing her thoughts via the written word. She loves local coffee shops, baking and spending time with family and friends.

Tami is wife to Todd and Mom to two grown children. She and her husband are recent empty nesters and are embracing this new season of life. Tami lives out her calling and purpose through her two home based businesses. She enjoys nature and walking, reading on her porch swing, sipping hot tea while watching her country sunset and spending time with family and friends.

Made in the USA
Monee, IL
03 May 2024

57762677R00115